Tom Hutchinson

...rter

new

HotLine

workbook

Oxford University Pres

OXFORD
UNIVERSITY PRESS

Great Clarendon Street, Oxford OX2 6DP

Oxford University Press is a department of the University of Oxford.
It furthers the University's objective of excellence in research, scholarship,
and education by publishing worldwide in

Oxford New York

Auckland Cape Town Dar es Salaam Hong Kong Karachi
Kuala Lumpur Madrid Melbourne Mexico City Nairobi
New Delhi Shanghai Taipei Toronto

With offices in

Argentina Austria Brazil Chile Czech Republic France Greece
Guatemala Hungary Italy Japan Poland Portugal Singapore
South Korea Switzerland Thailand Turkey Ukraine Vietnam

OXFORD and OXFORD ENGLISH are registered trade marks of
Oxford University Press in the UK and in certain other countries

© Oxford University Press 1998

The moral rights of the author have been asserted

Database right Oxford University Press (maker)

ISBN-13: 978 0 19 435756 2 (International edition)

First published 1998

2014 2013 2012 2011 2010
30 29 28 27 26 25 24 23 22 21

ISBN-13: 978 0 19 435913 9 (Turkish edition)

First published 1998

2004 2003 2002 2001 2000
10 9 8 7 6

Typeset by Tradespools Limited, Frome, Somerset

Printed in China

ACKNOWLEDGEMENTS

Designed by: Holdsworth Associates

The publishers would like to thank the Hamlyn
Publishing Group for permission to reproduce the
Top Ten Sports table from *Ordnance Survey National
Atlas of Great Britain* © The Hamlyn Publishing
Group Limited 1986.

*The publishers would like to thank the following for
permission to reproduce photographs:*
Camera Press (Colin Sted), Michael Cole
Camerawork, Format Photographers Ltd (Brenda
Prince/Melanie Friend), Sally and Richard
Greenhill, Robert Harding Picture Library, The
Kobal Collection.

Illustrations by: Anna Brookes, Stefan Chabluk,
Martin Cox, Suzanna English, Roger Fereday,
Phillip Gascoine, Jane Cedye, Clive Goodyer,
Sophie Harrison-Knibbs, Mac McIntosh.

Studio photography by: Garry and Marilyn O'Brien

Location photography by: Garry and Marilyn O'Brien;
John Walmsley

Introductions ▶1.1

1 Complete the speech bubbles.

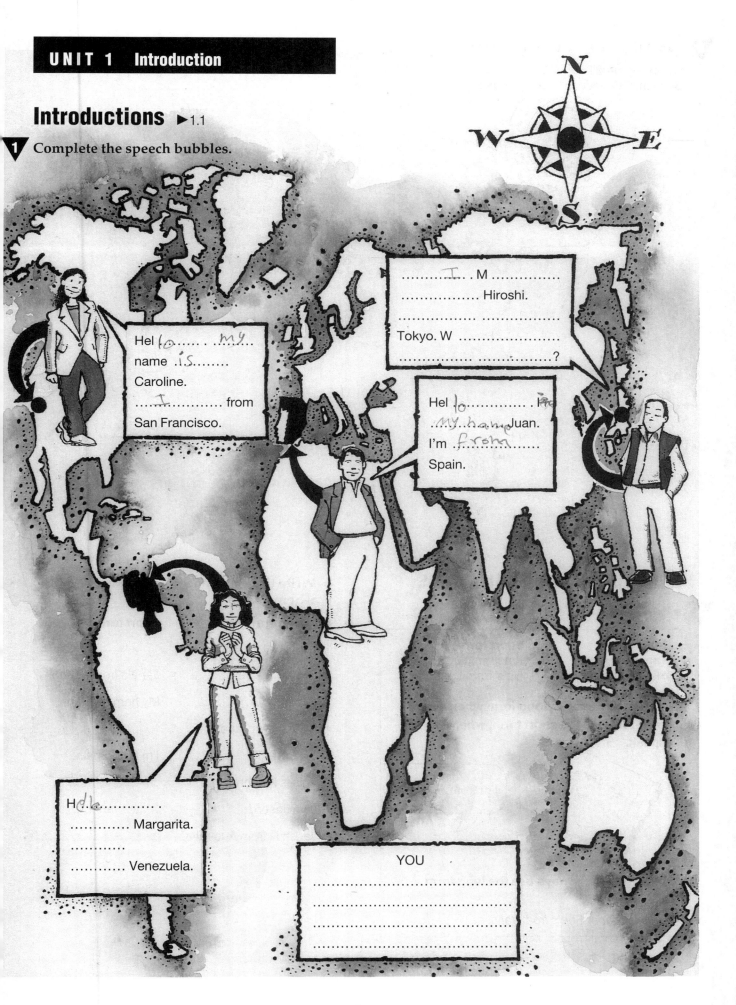

Hel lo...... my....
name .is........
Caroline.
.....I.......... from
San Francisco.

.... I . M ....
.... Hiroshi.
....
Tokyo. W ....
.....................................?

Hel lo............. i'm
.my ham.....Juan.
I'm from......
Spain.

H.e.l.o............ .
.... Margarita.
....
.... Venezuela.

YOU
....
....
....
....

Label these countries on the map.

Spain   Brazil   USA   Britain   France
Belgium Greece   Italy Russia

Long forms and short forms

 a Study these rules.

long form	short form
I **am** from Italy	I**'m** from Italy.
He **is** from London.	He**'s** from London.

We usually use the long form when we write. We use the short form, when we speak.

I am from Australia.

I'm from Australia.

With 'this' we always use the long form.

Example
*This **is** Maria. She's from Italy.*

b Write these sentences in the other form where possible.

long form	short form
1 I am from America.	....
2	Jane's from London.
3	My name's Alan.
4 She is from Japan.	....
5	I'm from Spain.
6 This is Madonna.	....
7 I am Jason.	....
8 Jason is from Australia.	....

Numbers 0–10

4 Complete this crossword with numbers 0–10.

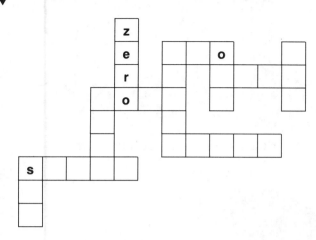

What's this?

5 Complete the speech bubbles. Use these words.

telephone   computer   pen   book
pizza   photograph

Example

What's this ?   It's a television .

1 .... ?    ....

2 .... ?    ....

3 .... ?    ....

4 .... ?    ....

5 .... ?    ....

6 .... ?    ....

Numbers 11–20

6 Write the numbers in full.

10 *ten*	16 ....
11	17 ....
12	18 ....
13	19 ....
14	20 ....
15	

his/her

7 a Study this rule.

What's **his** name?
His name's Stefan Edberg.

What's **her** name?
Her name's Steffi Graf.

We use 'his' for men and boys.
We use 'her' for women and girls.

b Complete these sentences with 'his' or 'her'.

1 This is Rebecca with .... MGB.

2 This is Stuart with .... Jaguar.

3 This is David. It's .... birthday today.

4 This is Jean. It's .... birthday today.

5 This is Cissy with .... boyfriend. What's .... name? John.

6 This is Paul with .... girlfriend. .... name's Julie.

8 ▼ **Look at this card. Complete the dialogue.**

> **Name** Helen Brown
>
> **Record for** boyfriend, John
>
> **Age** 17
>
> **Reason** birthday

DJ Hello. What's .... name?

Helen Helen Brown.

DJ Who is your .... for, Helen?

Helen .... for my boyfriend, John. It's .... birthday today.

DJ .... birthday, John. How old .... he?

Helen .... seventeen.

DJ Thank ...., Helen. Here's the record .... Helen and .... boyfriend, John.

Numbers 21–100

9 Write these numbers in full.

Example

76 *seventy-six*

39 ....

24 ....

100 ....

80 ....

99 ....

63 ....

41 ....

55 ....

70 ....

a/an ►1.2

10 **a Study this rule.**

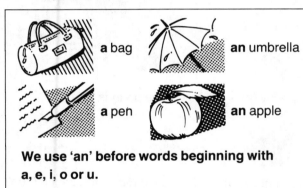

a bag **an** umbrella

a pen **an** apple

We use 'an' before words beginning with a, e, i, o or u.

b Write 'a' or 'an' in the space.

1 .... book

2 .... egg

3 .... orange

4 .... car

5 .... hamburger

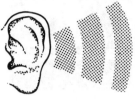

6 .... ear

7 .... cat

8 .... dog

9 .... arm

10 ...... insect

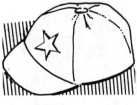

11 ...... hat

12 ...... astronaut

11 Complete this dialogue.

1. .... I .... you?

.... hamburger and .... fries, please.

2. .... else?

Yes .... orange .... , please.

3. .... £2.81, ...

.... you.

W O R D S N A K E

12 How many words can you find in this wordsnake?

Example
how   what   twenty

howhatwentyoumbrellappleightworangegirlfriendesknowholdoor

CULTURE SPOT

British money

a pound (£)

a penny (p)

five pounds (£5)

two pence (2p)

five pence (5p)

ten pence (10p)

twenty pence (20p)

fifty pence (50p)

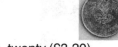
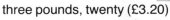

three pounds, twenty (£3.20)

How much money is there on this page altogether?

....

What is £1 worth in your currency?

....

VICTORIA ROAD

Introductions

1 Complete these dialogues.

Ⓐ1

.... do?

.... Simon.

Pleased ....,
Simon. My .... Josephine, but ....
.... Jo.

Ⓐ2

.... from, Jo?

New York. And you?

.... London.

Ⓑ1

Hello. .... your ....?

Rocard. Pierre Rocard.

Welcome to the International Centre.
.... Janet Swales.

How ...., Miss
Swales.

Ⓑ2

Oh, ... call me ....

Oh, well. .... meet ....,
Janet. .... name's Pierre.

The verb 'to be' ▶2.1

▼2 a Study this table.

I	am 'm	
He She	is 's	from America.
We You They	are 're	in the kitchen.

b Complete these dialogues with 'm, 's or 're.

1 Where are you from? — I........ from London.

2 Are Vince and Sue sixteen? — No, they........ fifteen.

3 How old is Casey? — He........ fifteen, too.

4 Look. You........ in this photograph. You........with Casey. — Oh, yes. We............ at the cafe.

5 Is this your Tina Turner record? — Yes. She........ my favourite pop star.

6 Kam. You........ my best friend. Am I bossy? — Well, yes, you are a bit bossy.

7 What are Casey and Kamala like? — They........ all right.

8 Where is Kamala from? — She........ from Britain.

9 Sue! Where are you? — I........ in the garden.

10 How old are you? — I........ fifteen. It........ my birthday today.

Possessive adjectives ▶2.4

▼3 Complete this list.

subject pronoun	possessive adjective
I	my
he	....
she	....
it	its
we	....
you	....
they	....

▼4 Complete what Casey says with these words.

girl	his	its	boy	best friend
Hi	our	friend	their	sister
twins	her	I'm	my	

1 H................ . ... name's Casey.
.... fifteen.

2 This is my .... , Vince. He's with his

.... name's Sue. They're

....

10

3 This .... is .... neighbour.
   .... name's Terry.

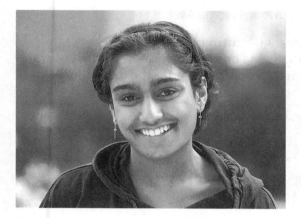

4 This .... is Kamala. Sue is her

   ....

5 This is .... street. .... name is
  Victoria Road.

The verb 'to be': negative ►2.2

5 **a** **Study this table.**

I	am not 'm not	
He She It	is not isn't	from America. Italian.
We You They	are not aren't	

b **Make these sentences negative.**

1 Boris Yeltsin is from America.

....

2 I'm from Hartfield.

....

3 Madrid and Barcelona are in Italy.

....

4 You're my best friend.

....

5 This car is a Jaguar.

....

6 I'm a Madonna fan.

....

7 Football is my favourite game.

....

8 We're from Victoria Road.

....

6 **Put these words in the correct column.**

OK	terrible	awful	great
wonderful	rubbish	not bad	

☺ good	😐 all right	☹ bad

The verb 'to be': questions ▶ 2.3

7 a Study these rules.

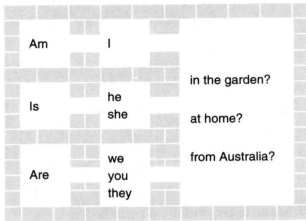

Am	I	
Is	he	in the garden?
	she	at home?
Are	we	from Australia?
	you	
	they	

> **To make questions with 'to be' we put the verb in front of the subject.**
>
> Example
> Jo ✕ is from America.
> *Is* ✕ *Jo from America?*

b Use the cues to complete the dialogues.

Example
Is this your new record? (this/your new record)
Yes, it is.

What's it like? (what/it like)
It's great.

1 Here's a postcard.

.... ? (Who/it from)

It's from Rebecca and John.

.... ? (they/on holiday)

Yes, they are.

.... ? (where/they)

They're in Italy.

2 .... ? (where/my pen)

I don't know. ....

.... ? (it/in your bag)

No, it isn't.

3 .... ? (where/you from)

I'm from England.

.... ? (you/from London)

No, I'm not. I'm from Liverpool.

4 .... ? (Terry/sixteen)

No, he isn't. He's fifteen.

.... ? (When/his birthday)

I don't know.

5 .... ? (Vince and Sue/in)

No, they aren't.

.... ? (Where/they)

They're at the leisure centre.

.... ? (they/with Casey)

Yes, they are.

.... ? (Where/the leisure centre)

It's in King George Avenue.

8 Kamala is joining the Guns 'n' Roses fan club. She is on the telephone now. Here are Kamala's answers. Write the questions.

.... ?

Kamala Wijeratne.

.... ?

W–I–J–E–R–A–T–N–E

.... ?

I'm 15.

.... ?

64 King George Avenue, Hartfield.

.... ?

It's 0326 791611.

Thank you. Welcome to the Guns 'n' Roses fan club.

Plurals ▶ 2.5

9 a Study these rules.

singular   plural

a book   two book**s**

a girl   three girl**s**

To make the plural we add -s.

These are irregular forms.
a man   two **men**
a woman   two **women**

b What can you see in the picture? Complete the list.

Examples
three pens   *a pencil*

....

....

....

....

....

Adjectives and nouns ▶2.7

10 a Study these rules.

> **The adjective goes in front of the noun.**
> **Adjectives do not change.**
>
> Examples
> | | **adjective** | **noun** |
> |------|---------------|----------|
> | *a* | *small* | *car* |
> | *a* | *black* | *pen* |
> | *two*| *black* | *pens* |
>
> **We use 'an' in front of an adjective beginning a, e, i, o or u.**
>
> Examples
> *a new car*   **an** *old car*

b Put the words in the correct order to make sentences.

1 my car is new this

....

2 great is Paul a singer McCartney

....

3 is large much a how hamburger

.... ?

4 T-shirts £6 the are each green

....

5 terrible a this book is

....

6 old where my is tracksuit

.... ?

7 they group an awful are

....

8 is friend Kamala good a

....

9 telephone number 629431 is our new

....

10 is group my favourite Dire Straits

....

INTERACTION

How much . . . ? ▶2.6

 Write the questions and answers.

Example

How much is this watch?
It's £20.

How much are these oranges?
They're 20p each.

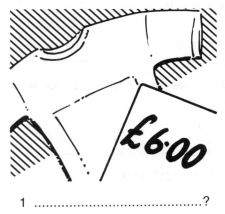

1 ....?

....

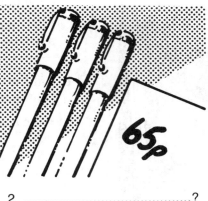

2 ....?

....

3 ....?

....

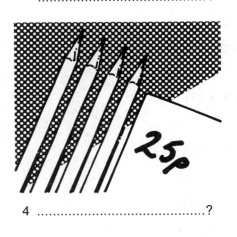

4 ....?

....

5 ....?

....

6 ....?

....

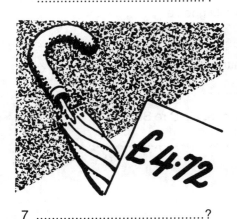

7 ....?

....

8 ....?

....

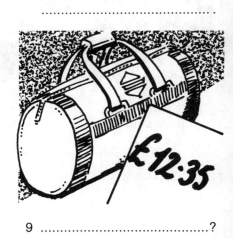

9 ....?

....

PROJECT

12 Find 5 more colours and 6 numbers.

K	Z	F	A	E	K	O	G	A	X	Z	M
D	T	A	O	R	M	Y	B	R	J	S	B
B	L	N	B	U	F	I	F	T	E	E	N
L	J	C	I	A	R	L	P	W	M	E	I
U	U	C	R	T	W	E	L	V	E	O	N
E	A	K	T	B	D	J	R	C	E	I	W
H	Y	E	L	L	O	W	V	A	I	O	T
B	Q	E	P	A	N	X	N	L	G	V	H
F	I	V	E	C	Y	G	F	S	H	H	R
U	G	Q	F	K	D	F	P	M	T	E	E
W	H	I	T	E	T	H	D	S	Y	G	E
K	B	Q	R	J	G	V	S	W	E	Y	X

We write addresses like this:

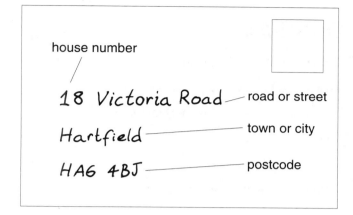

house number

18 Victoria Road — road or street

Hartfield — town or city

HA6 4BJ — postcode

We can use short forms of the names of roads.

Example

Victoria Road = *Victoria Rd*

Queen Street = *Queen St*

King George Avenue = *King George Ave*

CULTURE SPOT

Addresses

COMPARISON

How do you write addresses in your language?

First Class Mail

Miss Jill Langdon-Davis
33 Temple St
Oxford OX4 1JS

Oxford University Press
Walton Street, Oxford OX2 6DP

Ms Sara Gray
36 Beaumont Rd
Headington
Quarry
Oxford
OX3 8JN

Mr Brian Plater
12 Parsons Place
off Morrell Ave
Oxford

LEARNING DIARY

Self-check

1 Complete these dialogues.

1 Hello, Mrs Scott. .... Sue in?

Yes, she .... , Kamala. Sue! Where ....

you?

I.......... in the garden.

She.......... in the garden, Kamala.

2 Hello, Mrs Scott. .... Vince and Sue in?

Yes, they .... , Terry. Vince! Sue! Where

.... you?

We.......... in the kitchen.

They .... in the kitchen, Terry.

2 Make these sentences negative.

1 I'm sixteen.

....

2 We're from Australia.

....

3 Terry's our neighbour.

....

4 These apples are very good.

....

3 Complete this dialogue.

How .... badges?

They................. 20p ....

.... I .... two, please?

That's .... , please.

.... you are.

Thank you. .... 10p ....

.... you.

4 Describe these things. Use these words.

small   old   black   large

1 a ....

2 two ....

3 three ....

4 ....

5 Write 'this' or 'these'.

1 How much is .... cassette?

2 .... are my friends.

3 Are .... your books?

4 .... is our house.

6 Write the questions.

.... ?
Casey Royston.

.... ?
I'm fifteen.

.... ?
I'm from Hartfield.

Check your answers with a partner. If there is anything you do not understand, ask your teacher or check in the Grammar reference section on pages 109–114 of your Student's Book.

16

VICTORIA ROAD

Useful expressions

1 Complete the dialogue.

have/has got ▶3.1

2 **a** Study this table.

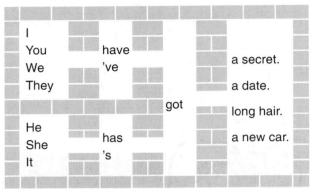

I You We They	have 've	got	a secret. a date. long hair. a new car.
He She It	has 's		

b Write 'have' or 'has'.

1 Darren .... got short hair.

2 He .... got a girlfriend.

3 They .... got a new neighbour.

4 I .... got an English book.

5 Sue .... got a brother.

6 We .... got a good teacher.

7 I .... got a new telephone number.

8 Terry .... got a date for Saturday.

9 Hartfield .... got a leisure centre.

10 You .... got my pen.

c Write the sentences with the short form of 'have' and 'has'.

1 ....

2 ....

3 ....

4 ....

5 ....

6 ....

7 ....

8 ....

9 ....

10 ....

have/has got: negative ▶3.1

3 **a** Study this table.

I You We They	have not haven't	got	blue eyes. short hair. a car.
He She It	has not hasn't		

b Make these sentences negative.

1 Terry's got a sister.

....

2 I've got twenty U2 records.

....

3 Tina Turner's got blonde hair.

....

4 Casey's got a new neighbour.

....

5 We've got a new car.

....

6 Clint Eastwood has got long hair.

....

7 Vince and Sue have got brown eyes.

....

8 I've got your bag.

....

9 Kamala's got a cat.

....

10 You've got a white T-shirt

....

4 **Write down:**

a **three things that you have got.**

Example
I've got a radio.

1 ....

2 ....

3 ....

b **three things that you haven't got.**

Example
I haven't got a computer.

1 ....

2 ....

3 ....

c **three things that your best friend has got.**

1 ....

2 ....

3 ....

d **three things that your best friend hasn't got.**

1 ....

2 ....

3 ....

READING

Genitives ▶ 3.3

5 **a** **Study these rules.**

This is Jane.

This is Jane**'s** car.

This is Alan.

These are Alan**'s** parents.

b **Whose is it?**

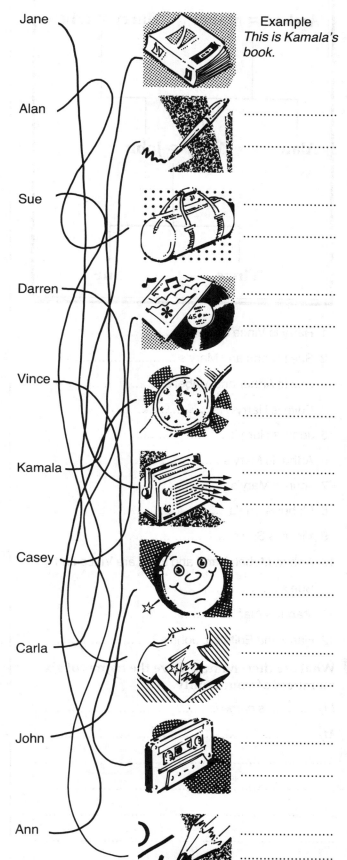

Jane
Alan
Sue
Darren
Vince
Kamala
Casey
Carla
John
Ann

Example
This is Kamala's book.

....

....

....

....

....

....

....

....

....

....

....

6 Look at this family tree. Complete the sentences with the correct word.

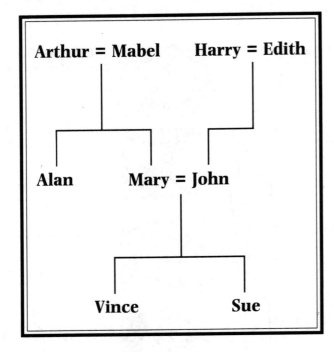

Arthur = Mabel   Harry = Edith

Alan   Mary = John

Vince   Sue

1 Harry is Vince's ....

2 Sue is John and Mary's ....

3 Sue is Arthur and Mabel's ....

4 Edith is Harry's ....

5 John is Harry's ....

6 Arthur is Mary's ....

7 John is Mary's ....

8 Mabel is Sue's ....

9 Vince is Sue's ....

10 Arthur, Mabel, Harry and Edith are Vince and Sue's ....

11 Mabel is Alan's ....

12 Harry and Edith are John's ....

 7 What are their names? Give the names of six members of your family.

My ....'s name is .... .

My .... .

....

....

....

....

 8 Complete the descriptions.

Carla

s............

bl............ h ....

br............ e ....

Sam

v............ t............

bl............ ....

bl............ ....

Jane and Joanne

t............

l............ f............ ....

gr............ ....

John

s............

s............ d............ ....

br............ ....

You

....

....

....

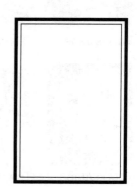

9 Describe the people in Exercise 8. Complete these descriptions.

Example

Carla is short. She has got black hair and brown eyes.

1 Sam .... very .... He ....
.... blond .... and ....
....

2 Jane and Joanne .... They
....
.... and ....

3 John ....
....
....

4 I ....
....
....

10 Describe your ideal date.

....
....
....
....

11 What are their jobs?

Example

aeioplcmn

He's a policeman.

rafbotoell

1 ....

croodt

2 ....

acreeth

3 ....

dettuns

4 ....

ereening

5 ....

gresni

6 ....

INTERACTION

have/has got: questions ▶3.2

 a Study these rules.

	I you we they		a sister?
Have		got	short hair?
			a date?
Has	he she it		a good job?

To make questions with 'have/has got' we put 'have' or 'has' in front of the subject.
We do not use short forms in questions.

In short answers, we do not say 'got'.

Example
Have you got a brother?
Yes, I have. (**Not** Yes, I have got.)
or *No, I haven't.* (**Not** No, I haven't got.)

b Jason and Angie are on a date. Jason is asking Angie some questions. Use these cues. Make his questions.

Example
Have you got a photograph of your family?
photograph of your family

1 .... ?
a car

2 .... ?
a good job

3 .... ?
a computer

4 .... ?
a brother or sister

5 .... ?
a stereo

6 .... ?
a best friend

7 .... ?
a favourite pop group

c Jason has got a sister. Angie is asking about her. Use these cues. Make her questions.

Example
Has she got long hair?
long hair

1 .... ?
a car

2 .... ?
a good job

3 .... ?
What colour eyes

4 .... ?
What colour hair

5 .... ?
a boyfriend

6 .... ?
a favourite pop group

PROJECT

Apostrophes ▶3.4

13 **a** Study these rules.

We use an apostrophe (') for genitives and short forms.

Example
Terry's date. **genitive**
She isn't here. **short form**

b Put in the apostrophes.

1 Ive got Janes book. Its in this bag.
2 How much are these postcards?
   Theyre 10p each.
3 Vinces dates Michaels cousin.
4 Whos this?
   Its Kamalas uncle.
5 Janes sisters are in these photographs.
6 Wheres my bag?
   I dont know. I havent got it.

CULTURE SPOT

Titles

Mr Smith /mɪstə/ **Mrs** Smith /mɪsɪz/

She is married.

Miss Smith /mɪs/ **Miss** Jones /mɪs/

They are not married.

We can use 'Ms' /məz/ instead of 'Mrs' or 'Miss'. We use 'Mr' and 'Ms' for married and unmarried men and women of any age.

Compare this to your own language.

LEARNING DIARY

Self-check

▼1 Complete this list.

male	female
grandfather	....
father	....
....	sister
....	wife
son	....
grandson	....

▼2 Look at this picture and complete what Ann says.

Hi. My .... Ann. I ....

.... fair .... and blue I

.... a brother, but I ....

.... a sister. My brother is very ....

He .... fair hair. He ....

.... short .... hair. My ....

name is Simon. He .... a job. He

.... student.

▼3 Here is part of an interview with Ann. Here are Ann's answers. What were the questions?

1 .... ?
Ann.

2 .... ?
Fair.

3 .... ?
Blue.

4 .... ?
I've got a brother but I haven't got a sister.

5 .... ?
Simon.

6 .... ?
No, he hasn't. It's dark.

7 .... ?
Brown.

Check your answers with a partner. If there is anything you do not understand, ask your teacher or check in the Grammar reference section on pages 109–114 of your Student's Book.

23

VICTORIA ROAD

Useful expressions

1 Complete the dialogues. Use these expressions.

Sorry!
Would you like to dance?
Excuse me. I can't see.

I'm sorry. I can't hear.
But I can't swim!
It's over there.

1 Where's London Road?

2 Go on.

3

4

5

6

LANGUAGE WORK

can/can't ►4.1

2 **a** **Study these rules.**

| I He She It We You They | can cannot can't | play the guitar. swim. speak. |

> 'Can't' is the short form of 'cannot'.
> 'Can' has no short form.

b **What can these people do? What can't they do?**

Example

He can play the piano.

She can't speak Chinese.

1 ....
....

2 ....
....

3 ....
....

4 ....
....

5 ....
....

6 ....
....

7 ....
....

8 ....
....

can/can't: questions ►4.2

 a Study these rules.

Can	I he she it we you they	play tennis? speak English? play the violin?

To make questions with 'can' we put 'can' in front of the subject.

Short answers
Yes, I can.
No, I can't.

b Look back at the pictures in Exercise 2. Make dialogues with the people in the pictures.

Example
Can you play the piano?
Yes, I can.

Can you speak Chinese?
No, I can't.

1 ....
   ....

2 ....
   ....

3 ....
   ....

4 ....
   ....

5 ....
   ....

6 ....
   ....

7 ....
   ....

8 ....
   ....

play

4 a Look.

I can play badminton. (sport)
I can play **the** piano. (musical instrument)

b What can Vince play? Use the words below.

guitar   basketball   violin   rugby   tennis

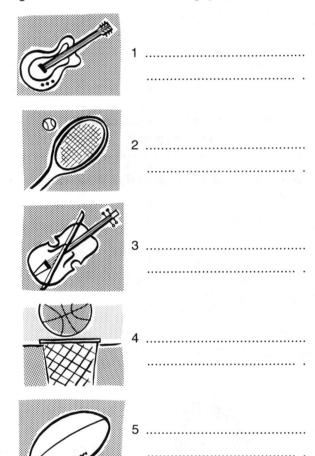

1 ....
   ....

2 ....
   ....

3 ....
   ....

4 ....
   ....

5 ....
   ....

5 Write down 5 things that you can do and 5 things that you can't do.

I can ....

I ....
   ....
   ....
   ....
   ....
   ....
   ....
   ....

READING

6 What subject is it?

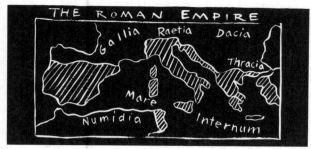

1 ....

2 ....

3 ....

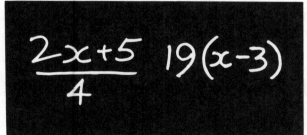

4 ....

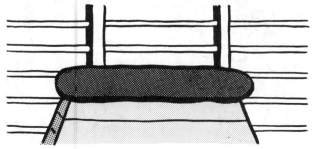

5 ....

6 ....

7 ....

8 ....

9 ....

10 ....

27

7 Which subjects do you like best? Write down all your school subjects in order from your favourite down to your least favourite.

....

....

....

....

....

....

....

....

....

....

8 Complete the diary page.

October 1991

6 _Monday_

7 ....

8 ....

9 ....

10 ....

11 ....

12 ....

LISTENING

9 Write the times under the watches and clocks.

1 ....

2 ....

3 ....

4 ....

5 ....

6 ....

7 ....

8 ....

9 ....

10 ....

10 Write this in the speech bubbles with the correct punctuation.

whatsthetime   itstenoclock

INTERACTION

on/at ►4.4

 11 a Study this rule.

We use 'on' with days.	We use 'at' with times.
Example	Example
on Wednesday	*at* five past eleven
on Saturday	*at* break

b Write the correct preposition.

.... nine o'clock .... lunchtime .... my birthday

.... Tuesday .... Sunday .... five to two

.... half past two

 12 Look at this invitation. Complete the conversation with these words.

Can	Bye	you	address
party	Thanks	o'clock	to
When	Saturday	Street	What
19	your	on	house	at

> ☞ **Come to the party**
> on Saturday at 8 o'clock
> ☆ at 19 Green Street
> *Hope you can come*
> ♥ *Jane*

Jane Hi.

Vince Hello, Jane.

Jane Can you come ...... my birthday ....?

Vince .... is it?

Jane It's .... Saturday.

Vince Is it at your ....?

Jane Yes, it is.

Vince OK. .... time?

Jane It's .... eight ....

Vince What's your ....?

Jane .... Green ....

Vince .... See .... on ....

Jane Yes. ...... you bring ...... Police records?

Vince OK. Bye.

Jane ....

13 Make the conversation for this invitation.

> ★ Party Invitation ★
> It's Casey's birthday
> on Friday at 7.30
> at 54 Victoria Road
> ★ *See you there* ★

....
....
....
....
....
....
....
....
....
....
....
....
....
....
....
....
....
....
....

14 Make your own party invitation.

PROJECT

Spelling

15 Some of these words are spelt wrongly. Write them correctly.

Histery	....
orange	....
Wendesday	....
seven, aight, nine	....
Munday	....
son and doughter	....
granfather	....
brown ayes	....
fair hair	....
Goegraphy	....
Inglish	....
apointment	....
guittar	....
football	....
fifty-too	....
birthday	....
qarter pas fife	....
sixtene	....
adres	....
cassette	....

Questions

16 Write the words in the correct order to make questions.

1 you musical can a play instrument

.... ?

2 are programmes favourite your TV what

.... ?

3 at subjects what good you are

.... ?

4 swim you can

.... ?

5 star is pop who favourite your

.... ?

CULTURE SPOT

The school day

The normal school day in Britain is from nine o'clock to half past three. Pupils must stay at school all the time.

The day starts with registration. The class teachers check who is at school and who is absent.

Then there is assembly. All the pupils come together for a religious service. The headmaster or headmistress reads out any important notices.

Lessons begin after assembly.

At lunchtime some pupils go home for lunch, but most pupils have their lunch at school.

The afternoon begins with registration again. School finishes at half past three.

Pupils don't go to school on Saturday or Sunday.

COMPARISON

Compare this to your country.
- What is your normal school day?
- Do you have registration and assembly?
- Where do you have lunch?

Self-check

1 Complete this conversation.

Girl Can I .... an .... for next Monday, please?

Receptionist I'm .... We aren't open .... Monday. .... you come .... Tuesday .... 10.30?

Girl No, I .... come .... the morning. .... you got an appointment .... the afternoon?

Receptionist Yes. Can you come .... two ....?

Girl Yes, OK.

2 Make dialogues. Use the words in brackets.

1 ....?
(swim you can)

  ....
(I can't no)

2 ....?
(the Vince guitar play can)

  ....
(can yes he)

3 What are these school subjects?

1 scumi .... 4 syothir ....

2 hayreggop .... 5 hrcnfe ....

3 shamt .... 6 lineghs ....

4 Write the times under the clocks.

1 ....
  ....

2 ....
  ....

3 ....
  ....

4 ....
  ....

5 ....
  ....

Check your answers with a partner. If there is anything you do not understand, ask your teacher or check in the Grammar reference section on pages 109–114 of your Student's Book.

VICTORIA ROAD

Useful expressions

1 Write these expressions in the correct speech bubbles.

And don't be late.
See you at the party tomorrow.
an appointment at the doctor's

I must go.
What's the time?
Yes, see you.

② Oh, ...

I've got ....

....

OK. ....

....

① ....

It's 6 o'clock.

Yes, OK. Nine o'clock at Jane's place.

Right. ....

....

③

All right.

See you.

....

32

Imperatives ►5.1

2 **a Study these rules.**

positive	negative

Sit down.	Don't sit down.
Stop.	Don't stop.

'Don't' is the short form of 'Do not'.

b Write these instructions in the correct place.

Get out of the way.
Please close the door.
Do not feed the animals.
Come here.
Do not touch.
Please put your trays here.
Don't open your eyes.
Read the instructions carefully.

1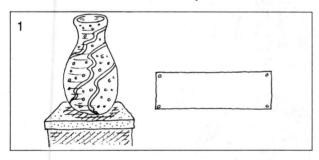

2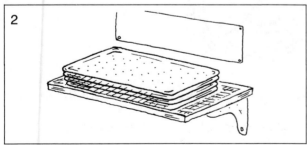

3

4

5

6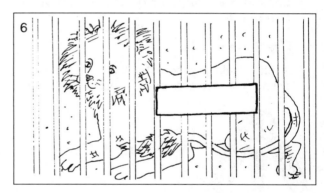

7

8

READING

must/mustn't ►5.2

a **Study these rules.**

I He She It We You They	must mustn't	stop. go. look.

Stop	Don't stop!
You **must** stop.	You **mustn't** stop.

'Mustn't' is the short form of 'must not'.

b **Look at these signs. Say what you must or mustn't do.**

Use these words.

| touch | take photographs | talk | smoke |
| swim | wear a seat belt | park | be careful |

1 ....

....

2 ....

....

3 ....

....

4 ....

....

5 ....

....

6 ....

....

7 ....

....

8 ....

....

4 **Complete these instructions with 'in' or 'on'.**

1 Don't keep disks .... the disk drive.

2 Don't write .... the envelope. Write .... the disk.

3 Don't put drinks .... the disks.

4 Don't keep disks .... the desk. Keep them .... their envelopes .... a box.

5 Don't put things .... the computer keyboard.

6 Don't keep disks .... a bag.

Yellow lines

5 Roads in Britain often have yellow lines. What do they mean? Match the instructions to the pictures.

You mustn't park here from 8 am to 6 pm.
You mustn't park here at any time.
You can park here at any time.
You can park here for 1 hour.

1 ....

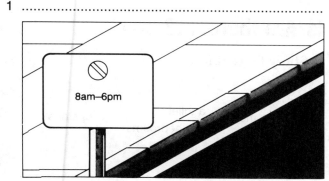

2 ....

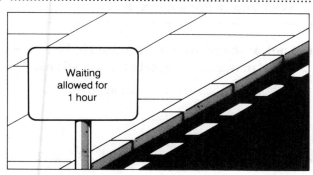

3 ....

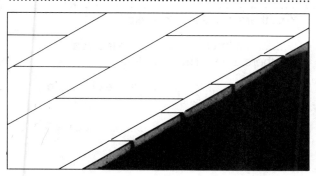

4 ....

W O R D S Q U A R E

6 Find ten more parts of a house in the wordsquare.

O	T	D	J	B	K	A	O	D	J	C	W
S	G	O	L	C	O	E	E	O	H	P	I
A	A	P	I	N	I	G	M	W	Q	U	N
N	R	B	F	L	A	G	T	N	F	E	D
Y	D	M	G	R	E	P	D	S	E	B	O
K	E	L	A	F	Q	T	H	T	R	E	W
R	N	G	C	U	P	B	O	A	R	D	H
X	Q	G	B	V	D	V	F	I	M	R	S
D	O	O	R	H	I	R	C	R	X	O	E
C	K	I	T	C	H	E	N	S	G	O	N
W	J	W	A	U	L	Z	D	K	T	M	I
B	A	T	H	R	O	O	M	Y	L	O	O

there is/are ►5.3

7 **a** Study these rules.

	is		
	's	a bathroom	
	isn't		
There			upstairs.
	are		
	aren't	two bathrooms	

We do not use a short form with 'There are'.

Example
There is a book on the table.
There's a book on the table.
or
There are two books on the table.
(**But not**
There're two books on the table.)

35

b Look at this picture. Complete the sentences.

Example
There's a computer on the desk.

1 .... three books
   ....

2 .... a pen
   ....

3 .... four pencils
   ....

4 .... a disk
   in ....

5 .... a disk drive
   ....

6 .... two disks
   ....

7 .... a drink near
   ....

8 .... a book
   .... the chair.

9 .... two bags
   ....

10 .... three records
   ....

8 Describe your house or flat. Use 'There is', 'There are' or 'There isn't'.

Example
There are five rooms in our house.
There isn't a garage. (garage)

1 .... rooms in our ....

2 .... (kitchen)

3 .... (garage)

4 .... (toilet)

5 .... (bathroom)

6 .... (bedroom)

7 .... (cellar)

8 .... (garden)

9 .... (dining room)

10 .... (cupboards)

Is/Are there. . .? ►5.3

9 **a** Study these rules.

Is	there	a toilet	upstairs?
Are		two bedrooms	

> **To make questions with 'there is/are' we put 'Is' or 'Are' in front of 'there'.**

b Look at the picture in Exercise 7b. Here are some answers. Complete the questions.

1 .... a computer
   ....?
   Yes, there is.

2 How many bags ....?
   Two.

3 .... on the desk?
   Yes, there is. It's a milk shake.

4 .... three .... on the desk?
   No, there aren't. There are four.

5 .... in the disk drive?
   Yes, there is.

6 How many .... bag?
   Three.

36

Requests

10 Match these dialogues to the pictures.

OK. Give it to me.	Yes, OK.
Why can't you do it?	Yes, if I see her.

Can you help with the housework?
Can you carry this bag for me, please?
Can you close the door, please?
Can you wait for me?
Can you give this book to Carol?
I'm sorry. I must do my homework.
I'm sorry. I'm in a hurry.
Can you open the door for me, please?

Wordbuilding: front and back

11 a Complete the labels.

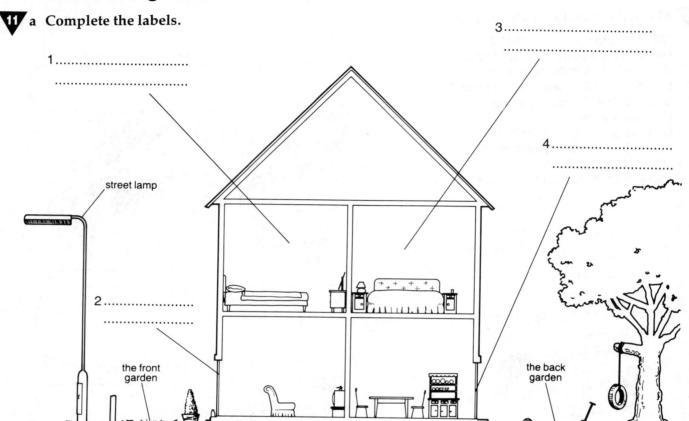

3 ....
....

1 ....
....

street lamp

4 ....
....

2 ....
....

the front
garden

the back
garden

The living room window

b Complete the labels.

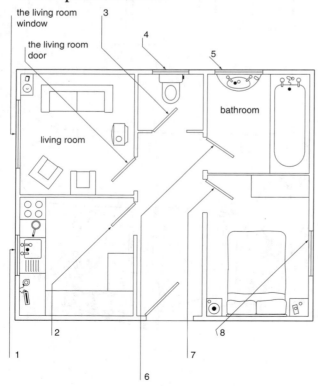

the living room
window   3

the living room
door   4

5

bathroom

living room

2

1

6

7

8

Describing a room

12 Look at the plan of a house in Exercise 11b.
Complete this description of the living room
with these items.

are two	next to the
window	a television
small	the garden
are	the back of
on the	the window
there's a	

The living room is .... kitchen. It's at

.... the house. It's got one

.... From the window you can see

.... The walls .... white

and .... blue carpet ....

floor. There .... armchairs and a settee

in the room. There's also .... and

there's a .... table near

....

Houses

Most people in Britain live in houses, not flats.

Usually only one family lives in one house.

A typical house has got two floors. The kitchen and the living room are downstairs. Some houses have a dining room downstairs, too.

Upstairs there are two, three or four bedrooms and a bathroom. The toilet is usually in the bathroom. A lot of houses have another toilet downstairs.

Most houses have a back garden and a lot also have a front garden.

There are different kinds of houses.

These are terraced houses.

This is a detached house.

These are semi-detached houses.

COMPARISON

- What are typical houses or flats like in your country?
- Compare them to the houses above.

Self-check

1 Label these pictures.

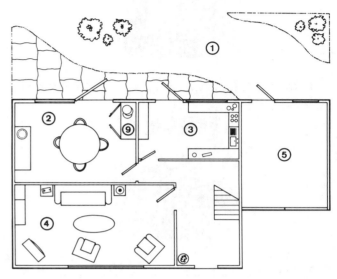

GROUND FLOOR

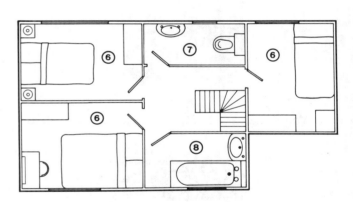

FIRST FLOOR

1	6 ....
2	7 ....
3	8 ....
4	9 ....
5	

2 Complete these dialogues about the house.

.... a garden?

.... a back garden, but

.... a front garden.

How many bedrooms ....?

.... three bedrooms upstairs.

3 ▼ Complete the sentences.

1 You .... smoke here.

2 You .... here.

3 You .... careful.

4 You .... here.

4 ▼ What are these people saying?

1 (D.. .)

2 (.... the window .)

3 (L.. at that .)

4 (Please ....)

Check your answers with a partner. If there is anything you do not understand, ask your teacher or check in the Grammar reference section on pages 109–114 of your Student's Book.

Revision crossword

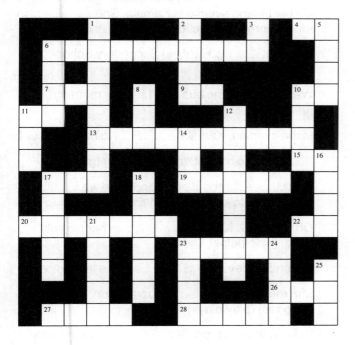

Clues

ACROSS

4 ____ Tuesday
6 Vince and Sue are Terry's ____ .
7 Don't = Do ____ .
9 How do you ____ .
10 Don't ____ silly!
11 This is Casey. ____'s from Victoria Road.
13 the opposite of 'upstairs'
15 What are you up ____?
17 Get out of the ____ .
19 4 + 4 = ?
20 Geography is a school ____.
22 How do you say 'hello' ____ French?
23 Blue + yellow = ____.
26 A Jaguar is a fast ____.
27 Pleased to ____ you.
28 the opposite of 'small'

DOWN

1 Happy ____!
2 the opposite of 'bad'
3 ____ this your pen?
5 What's your ____?
6 ____, ten, eleven
8 ____ old are you?
10 Kamala is Sue's ____ friend.
11 What colour eyes ____ she got?
12 son and ____
14 Where's Jane? ____'s in the kitchen.
16 Please ____ the window.
17 ____ you like to dance?
18 ____ me. Where's the loo?
21 Can I have an orange ____, please?
23 boy and ____
24 good
25 Where ____ you from?

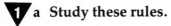

UNIT 7 Sport

VICTORIA ROAD
The present simple tense ►7.1

1 a Study these rules.

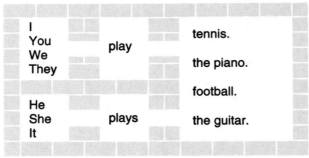

I			
You	play		tennis.
We			the piano.
They			football.
He			
She	plays		the guitar.
It			

We add -s to the verb in the third person singular.

Example
*Terry **lives** in Victoria Road.*
*He **plays** table tennis.*

Note these two verbs.

I go to school at 8 o'clock.
She go**es** to school at 8 o'clock.

I do my homework on Saturday.
He do**es** /dʌz/ his homework on Saturday.

The present simple tense describes regular activities.

---

b Complete these sentences with 'play' or 'plays'.

1 Kamala .... the piano.

2 Casey and Vince .... football.

3 Vince .... the guitar.

4 Terry .... table tennis.

5 Sue and Kamala .... badminton.

6 Casey .... tennis.

c What do you play? Complete these about yourself and your friends.

1 I ....

2 My best friend and I ....

3 My best friend ....

2 Complete this text. Choose the correct word from the brackets.

My name's Sue. I .... in Victoria Road. (live/lives)

My best friend's name is Kamala. She .... in King George Avenue. (live/lives)

We .... to Hartfield Secondary School. (go/goes)

We .... the bus at 8.15 every morning. (get/gets)

In the evening, Kamala .... to my house or I .... to her flat. (come/comes) (go/goes)

We .... about our friends and we .... to records. (talk/talks) (listen/listens)

On Saturday, Kamala .... in her parents' shop. (help/helps)

But on Sunday, she .... to the leisure centre with me and we .... badminton. (go/goes) (play/plays)

Kamala is very good. She .... for the school team. (play/plays)

Sometimes my brother Vince .... with us. (come/comes)

After badminton, we .... to the cafe. (go/goes)

We .... a drink and we .... our friends. (have/has) (meet/meets)

The present simple tense: -es endings ►7.1

3 **a** Study these rules.

> **When verbs end in -sh, -ch or -ss,**
> **we add -es in the 3rd person singular.**
> **We pronounce the -es /ɪz/.**
>
> Example
> I finish /fɪnɪʃ/   I miss /mɪs/
> *He finishes* /fɪnɪʃɪz/   *He misses* /mɪsɪz/
> I watch /wɒtʃ/
> *She watches* /wɒtʃɪz/
>
> **When the verb ends in -se /s/ or /z/,**
> **we add -s in the 3rd person singular.**
> **We pronounce the -es /ɪz/.**
>
> Example
> I practise /præktɪs/   I choose /tʃuːz/
> *She practises* /præktɪsɪz/ *She chooses* /tʃuːzɪz/

Vince's day

b Describe Vince's day. Use the cues below.

watch TV   practise the guitar
come home   have his breakfast
finish his homework   catch the bus
have dinner   do his homework
get up   start school
go to bed

Example

*He gets up at half
past seven.*

1 ....

....

2 ....

....

3 ....

....

4 ....

....

5 ....

....

6 ....

....

7 ....

....

8 ....

....

9 ....

....

10 ....

....

▼4 Describe your day.

....
....
....
....
....
....
....
....
....
....

▼5 Complete these sentences.

1 I get .... at 10 o'clock .... the morning.

2 Terry goes .... school .... his friends.

3 Mr Scott comes home 6.30

.... Monday .... Friday.

4 Casey lives .... Victoria Road .... number 64.

5 Bobby Best goes .... with his girlfriend

.... Sunday.

6 Mrs Scott works .... a shop .... Hartfield.

7 Would you like .... see a video .... my birthday?

8 I must stay in bed .... the rest .... the day.

LISTENING

The present simple tense: negative ►7.2

▼6 a Study these rules.

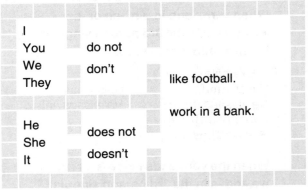

| I / You / We / They | do not / don't | like football. |
| He / She / It | does not / doesn't | work in a bank. |

To make the present simple negative we put 'don't' or 'doesn't' in front of the verb.
In the third person there is no -s on the verb. The -s is on 'does'.

Example
He doesn't **live** in this street.
He **lives** in Victoria Road.
She doesn't **watch** football matches.
She **watches** television.

b Write 'don't or 'doesn't'.

1 Bobby Best .... play for Liverpool.

2 He .... go to work on Sunday.

3 Bobby and his girlfriend .... go out on Monday.

4 The players .... go to the club on Monday.

5 They .... get up early on Monday.

6 The players .... practise in the afternoon.

7 The manager .... choose the new team till Thursday afternoon.

8 Bobby's girlfriend .... work on Saturdays.

9 She .... watch the match.

10 The players .... eat lunch before the match.

7 One of Darren Tooley's friends is talking, but all the information is wrong. Correct the sentences.

Example
We want Casey Royston.
We don't want Casey Royston. We want Terry Moore.

1 Terry lives in King Edward Avenue.

....

....

2 Terry goes to school by car.

....

....

3 Terry and his friends get the 8.30 bus.

....

....

4 They come home at six o'clock.

....

....

5 Terry plays football on Wednesdays.

....

....

6 Terry comes home late on Tuesdays.

....

....

7 Terry's friends come home late on Wednesday.

....

....

Your life

8 Write full sentences.

Example
a pop star that you don't like
I don't like Michael Jackson.

a sport that you don't play

I ....

a TV programme that you don't watch

I ....

something that you don't do on Sundays

I ....

something that your mother doesn't like

She ....

something that your father doesn't like

He ....

something that you don't do in the morning

I ....

something that you don't do in the evening

I ....

in/on/at ▶4.4

9 a Study these rules.

We use 'in' with parts of the day. Example *in* the evening (but note: **at** night) **We use 'at' with times.** Example *at* 10 o'clock **We use 'on' with days.** Example *on* Tuesday

b Write the correct preposition.

1 .... two o'clock

2 .... the morning

3 .... 9.30

4 .... Wednesday

5 .... the evening

6 .... Saturday

7 .... quarter past three

8 .... night

9 .... 2.15

10 .... Friday

11 .... the afternoon

The present simple tense: questions ►7.3

 a Study these rules.

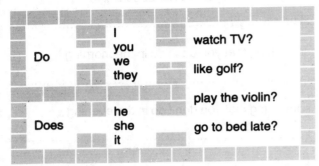

To ask questions in the present simple, we put 'do' or 'does' in front of the subject.

Example
I work in a bank.
Do you work in a bank?
Where do you work?

In the third person there is no -s on the end of the verb. The -s is on 'does'.

Example
She **lives** in Victoria Road.
Does she **live** *in Victoria Road?*

The manager **watches** the players.
When does the manager **watch** *the players?*

b Write 'do' or 'does'.

1 Excuse me. .... you live in this street?

2 .... you know Sue Scott?

3 .... she live in this street?

4 What number .... she live at?

5 .... Sue play tennis?

6 Where .... Sue and Kamala play badminton?

7 What time .... Sue and Vince go to school?

8 .... they go by car?

9 .... Terry go with them?

10 When .... they come home?

11 The interviewer is asking Karen some questions. Here are Karen's answers. Use the cues to make the questions.

1 (When/you/get up)

.... ?
At four o'clock in the morning.

2 (When/you/practise)

.... ?
From five o'clock to eight o'clock.

3 (Where/you/practise)

.... ?
At Streatham skating rink.

4 (your mother/take you to the rink)

.... ?
No, she doesn't. My father takes me.

5 (he/watch you)

.... ?
No, he doesn't. He goes to work.

6 (Where/he/work)

.... ?
He works in London.

7 (What/he/do)

.... ?
He drives a taxi.

8 (other skaters/practise with you)

.... ?
Yes. Two boys and another girl.

9 (they/practise every day, too)

.... ?
Yes, they do.

10 (When/you go out with your friends)

.... ?
On Saturdays, but I come home at nine o'clock.

12 Match the opposites.

upstairs	terrible
start	late
old	small
black	fair
early	sit
stand	short
large	white
good	finish
wonderful	downstairs
dark	bad
long	new

Sports survey

13 **a** **Complete the labels in the graph.**

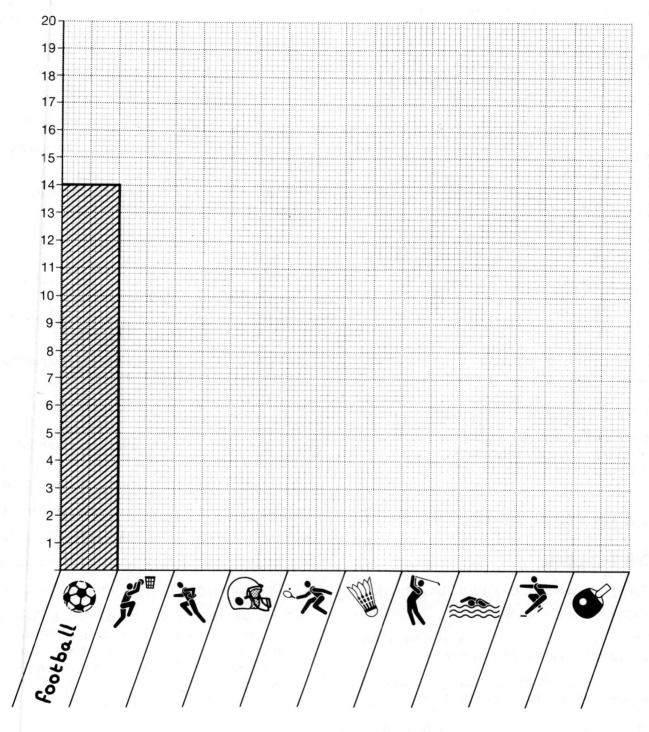

b Read the text and complete the graph.

These are the results of our sports survey. First, team sports: fourteen people play football; six people play rugby, two people play basketball and one person plays American football.

Now, individual sports: twelve people play tennis, four people play badminton and three people play table tennis. Eight people go swimming; two people go ice skating and only one person plays golf.

CULTURE SPOT

Popular sports

These are the popular sports in Britain.

TOP TEN SPORTS – of people that watch sport on television, percentage interested (based on household survey 1984)					
Men		**%**	**Women**		**%**
1	Snooker	76	**1**	Tennis	56
2	Football	69		Skating	56
3	Athletics	52	**3**	Snooker	52
	Boxing	52	**4**	Athletics	47
5	Motor car racing	49	**5**	Show jumping	46
	Tennis	49	**6**	Swimming	36
7	Cricket	47	**7**	Snow sports	35
	Darts	47	**8**	Darts	34
9	Golf	42	**9**	Football	33
10	Rugby Union	40	**10**	Golf	23

COMPARISON

Compare this list to your country.
- What are the popular sports in your country?
- Are there any sports here that you don't know?

LEARNING DIARY

Self-check

1 Complete this text. Use the verbs in brackets.

Trevor Barnes is a DJ. He .... for Radio 581. (work) He .... the Late Night Music Programme. (present) On his programme, he

.... records and .... to people on the telephone. (play/talk)

This is his day. 'I .... at 8 o'clock in the evening. (get up)

At half past nine I .... to the radio station. (drive) I .... work at half past ten. (start)

The programme .... at 1 o'clock in the morning. (start) It .... at 4 o'clock.

(finish) I .... home then. (not go) I .... a break from 4.00 till 5.30. (take)

Then I .... the producer. (meet) We .... about the next day's programme.

(talk) I .... the records. (not choose) The producer .... them. (choose) I .... home at 7 o'clock. (go)' Trevor .... to bed in the morning. (not go) He .... golf or .... a video. (play/ watch) He .... to bed at 1 o'clock in the afternoon. (go)

2 Here is part of an interview with Trevor. Complete the questions.

1 When ....?
At 8 o'clock.

2 When ....?
At 1 o'clock in the morning.

3 .... the records?
No, I don't. The producer chooses them.

4 What .... on your programme?
I play records and I talk to people.

·5 What time ....?
At four o'clock in the morning.

3 Use the verbs. Make true statements about Trevor's day.

1 Trevor .... in the afternoon. (work)

2 Trevor .... the records. (choose)

3 'I .... a break till 4.00.' (take)

4 'I .... tennis.' (play)

5 The programme .... at 12 o'clock. (start)

Check your answers with a partner. If there is anything you do not understand, ask your teacher or check in the Grammar reference section on pages 109–114 of your Student's Book.

VICTORIA ROAD

want to

1 **a Look.**

I **want to** catch the bus.
Do you want to join us?
I **don't want to** take my bag to the cinema.
She **doesn't want to** play tennis.
She **wants to** listen to records.

b Look at the pictures. What don't the people want to do? What do they want to do?

Use the cues below.

go to school	drive a fast car
stay in bed	go to a party
watch TV	be a rock and roll singer
help with the housework	get up
go skiing	work in a shop
wash the car	play football
do his homework	catch the bus

Example
I don't want to go to school.
I want to go skiing.

1 He...

....

2 She...

....

3 I...

....

4 He...

....

5 He...

....

6 I...

....

2 What do you want to do in your life?
Write down four things that you want to do.
Write four things that you don't want to do.

....

....

....

....

....

....

....

....

Object pronouns ▶8.1

3 **a** Look.

subject	verb	object	subject	verb	object
Sue	knows	Terry.	Terry	knows	Sue.
She	knows	him.	He	knows	her.

These are subject pronouns.	These are object pronouns.
I	me
you	you
he	him
she	her
it	it
we	us
they	them

b Write the correct pronoun.

1   I love ...., but do you love ....?

No, ... don't.

2   This is my new coat. Do you like ....?

Yes, ...'s very nice

3   Does Terry Moore live here?

I'm sorry. I don't know ....

4   That's Vince's new girlfriend. Do you like ....?

Yes, ...'s nice.

5   Where are my U2 records?

.... don't know. I haven't got .... Are .... in your room?

6   We play American football on Sunday. Why don't you join ....? .... start at 10 o'clock.

READING

The leisure centre

▼ 4 a Read this poster.

**Come to
Hartfield leisure centre**

for sport

for entertainment

There's a disco
every Saturday

We show films on
Tuesday and Thursday

There's a restaurant and cafe, too

You can have a great time at Hartfield
leisure centre

We're open 8am–11pm every day

Join today

b What can you do at the leisure centre?
Make dialogues. Use these cues.

play football dance
go skiing   watch films
buy clothes go windsurfing
have a meal play table tennis
go swimming go ice-skating

 Example
Can you play football there?
Yes, you can.

Can you go skiing there?
No, you can't.

.... ?
....
.... ?
....
.... ?
....
.... ?
....
.... ?
....
.... ?
....
.... ?
....

Silent letters

▼ 5 A lot of words in English have got a silent
letter. You don't hear it. What is the missing
letter in these words?

s__ience g__itar programm__

girlfr__end cu__board __now

sc__ool su__prise w__ite

__ho w__at he__vy

wa__k bre__kfast __rite

__rong i__land We__nesday

51

6 Find ten more places in the wordsquare.

R	I	S	L	A	N	D	I	D	R	T	P
F	C	Q	P	F	M	E	P	Q	E	C	O
B	O	S	S	H	O	P	R	K	S	D	S
H	O	R	A	H	A	E	R	Y	T	S	T
S	G	C	E	R	J	A	F	T	A	D	O
B	A	J	G	S	M	G	X	B	U	B	F
H	T	P	V	R	T	V	W	O	R	W	F
K	A	B	E	A	C	H	T	N	A	N	I
I	L	P	K	N	J	I	M	X	N	A	C
I	U	L	C	Y	Z	L	L	O	T	Q	E
S	K	M	V	I	L	L	A	G	E	F	V
C	I	N	E	M	A	U	E	M	S	E	A

7 Look at these dialogues. Where are the people? Use the words below.

restaurant   tennis court   post office
supermarket   beach   cinema
swimming pool   disco   souvenir shop
museum

Example

> Would you like to dance?

> Yes, OK.

They're at the disco.

> Can I send these two letters to America, please?

1 ....

> Can I help you?

> Yes, two hamburgers, please.

2 ....

> How much is this watch?

> It's £20.

3 ....

> Isn't this a good film?

> Yes, it's great.

> Ssh!

> Sorry.

4 ....

> Thirty–fifteen.

> Never! It's forty–love.

> No, it isn't. It's thirty–fifteen

5 ....

> Look at these old cars.

> Yes. Aren't they fantastic?

6 ....

> Let's go to the beach.

> No. I want to swim here.

7 ....

> How much are these apples?

> They're 10p each.

8 ....

> Look. Is that John?

> Where?

> There in the sea.

9 ....

LISTENING

 8 Put these words in the correct column.

lion	castle	house	forest	shop
hill	beach	river	dog	snake
hut	sea	tiger	cat	cinema
insect	church	island	horse	supermarket
spider	hospital			

animal	building	natural feature
lion	*castle*	*forest*

Plurals with -es ►2.5

 9 a Study this rule.

singular	plural

a beach   two beach**es**

an address   two address**es**

When words end with -ch /tʃ/ **-s** /s/ **or -sh** /ʃ/
we pronounce the -es /ɪz/.

b Complete the table.

singular	plural
a beach	two ....
an address	....
a forest	....
a lion	....
a watch	....
a letter	....
a bank	....
a hut	....
a princess	....
a church	....
a castle	....
a bus	....
a photograph	....
an insect	....

some/any ►8.3

10 a Study these rules.

> **We use 'some' with positive statements.**
>   Example
>   *I've got* **some** *photographs.*
>
> **We use 'any' with negative statements.**
>   Example
>   *I haven't got* **any** *photographs.*
>
> **We use 'any' with questions.**
>   Example
>   *Have you got* **any** *photographs?*

b Complete these sentences with 'some' or 'any'.

1 We've got .... new neighbours.

2 Have you got .... change?

3 I've got .... photographs of my holiday.

4 There aren't .... cars on the island.

5 There are .... nice things in the souvenir shop.

6 Are there .... telephones near here?

7 I haven't got .... friends.

8 I need .... new clothes.

At the shop

11 **a** Look at this shopping list.

pens

postcards

badges

videos

films

envelopes

cassettes

apples

oranges

eggs

b Look at the shop. Have they got the things?

Example
They haven't got any pens.
They've got some postcards.

....

....

....

....

....

....

....

c Make the dialogues in the shop.

Example
Have you got any pens?
No, I'm sorry. We haven't.

Have you got any postcards?
Yes, we have. How many do you want?

.... ?

....

.... ?

....

.... ?

....

.... ?

....

.... ?

....

.... ?

....

.... ?

INTERACTION

Making and refusing suggestions

12 **a** Look.

Would you like to dance?

I'm sorry, I can't. I'm here with my boyfriend.

2 ....
....
....
....

b Write the dialogues. Use these cues for the suggestions.

have a drink	go to the leisure centre
read this book	listen to my new cassette
play badminton	see our new car
go shopping	look at my photographs
go to the cafe	come to my party

Choose the answers from this list.

I'm sorry. I haven't got time.
I'm sorry. I must go. I've got an appointment at the doctor's.
I'm sorry. I must go to my grandparents'.

3 ....
....
....
....

1 ....
....
....
....

4 ....
....
....
....

5 ....
....
....
....

8 ....
....
....
....

6 ....
....
....
....

9 ....
....
....
....

7 ....
....
....
....

10 ....
....
....
....

Making arrangements

▼**13** **a** Complete this conversation.

Let's go .... the disco.

OK. What time .... it start?

Half .... nine.

What time must .... meet?

Quarter past nine, I think.

OK. See you .... the leisure centre ....

quarter past nine.

Fine. See ....

b Make new dialogues. Use these cues.

football match/2 o'clock/1 o'clock/club
pop concert/9 o'clock/8 o'clock/theatre

1 ....
....
....
....
....
....
....
....
....

2 ....
....
....
....
....
....
....
....
....

PROJECT

A postcard

▼**14** Complete the postcard.

POSTCARD

_____ Vince and Sue

We're _____ holiday _____ Spain. The

hotel _____ wonderful and _____ are

lots of things to do. You _____ play tennis.

You can swim _____ the sea or in the pool.

_____ the moment we're _____ the beach.

_____ beautiful. Hope you _____ well. Bye

_____ Rebecca and Alan

W O R D C I R C L E

▼**15** How many words can you find in the
wordcircle? Write them below.

....
....
....
....
....
....
....

CULTURE SPOT

Community work

A lot of young people in Britain do community work as part of their school work. They work for one or two afternoons a week. Sometimes they do community work on Saturday mornings, too.

They do a lot of different things. Some help old people or disabled people. They go shopping for them, iron clothes or wash up.

If the old person can't see very well, the girl or boy reads the newspaper or magazine to them.

Some young people help in hospitals or in children's homes.

COMPARISON

Compare this to your country. Do young people in your country do community work?

LEARNING DIARY

Self-check

1 Write the correct pronoun.

1 Tell Sue and Vince about the party, if you see ....

2 Is Terry here? We want ....

.... 'm sorry. .... isn't here.

3 Look. There's Jane Fox.

Where? I can't see ....

.... 's over there near that red car.

4 Kam and I want to go to the station, Dad. Can .... take .... in the car?

2 Write 'some' or 'any'.

1 Have you got .... Wet Wet Wet records?

We haven't got .... records, but there are .... cassettes over there by the window.

2 They've got .... new things at the shop.

Have they got .... pens?

Yes, they've got .... nice ballpoint pens.

3 I can't go to the dance. I haven't got .... money.

3 Complete these sentences with 'in', 'on', 'at' or 'to'.

1 Let's go .... the disco .... Friday.

OK. See you .... nine o'clock .... the disco.

2 There aren't any cars .... the island.

3 .... the morning we go .... the beach.

4 Let's have a picnic .... the forest.

5 We have lunch .... the restaurant every day.

6 There isn't a bathroom .... our hut.

7 Can you buy clothes .... the shop?

8 You can fish .... the river.

9 There aren't any sharks .... the sea here.

10 There's nobody .... home .... the evening.

11 There are a lot of insects in the huts .... night.

Check your answers with a partner. If there is anything you do not understand, ask your teacher or check in the Grammar reference section on pages 109–114 of your Student's Book.

58

VICTORIA ROAD

Useful expressions

1 Complete the dialogue with the expressions below.

What's the matter
I've got an appointment
See you.
round the corner
Wait a minute

I can't explain
at the hospital
I'm in a hurry
Where are you going
I'm late

3

But the doctor's is only ....
....

1

....,
Rebecca.

I'm, sorry. I can't stop. ....
....

2

Why? ....
........................?

....
with the doctor and ....

I've got an appointment ....
....

4

Why? ....
........................?

....
now. ....

59

The present continuous tense ►9.1

 a Study these rules.

I	am 'm am not 'm not	going to the shops.
He She It	is 's is not isn't	waiting for the bus. wearing blue trousers.
We You They	are 're are not 're not	carrying Sue's bags.

We make the present continuous with the verb 'to be' and a present participle.
The present continuous tense describes what is happening now.

b Put the verb in brackets into the present continuous tense.

Example
Sue is waiting for a bus.

1 We .... to the cinema. (go)

2 Vince and Casey .... football. (play)

3 I .... a hamburger. (eat)

4 You .... my milkshake. (drink)

5 Terry .... a green sweater. (wear)

c Make the sentences negative.

Example
Sue isn't waiting for a bus.

1 ....

2 ....

3 ....

4 ....

5 ....

Present participles: spelling

 a Study these rules.

To make the present participle we add -ing.
Example
go *going*   eat *eating*

When the verb ends in -e, we drop the -e and add -ing.
Example
come *coming*   have *having*

When the verb has a short vowel and one consonant, we double the consonant and add -ing.
Example
sit *sitting*   put *putting*

b Make the present participles of these verbs.

swim ....   speak ....

do ....   write ....

wait ....   watch ....

sing ....   miss ....

get ....   choose ....

drive ....

4 Some people are looking at their holiday photographs. Complete the dialogues with the verbs in brackets.

Example
Look. We'*re having* lunch at the Blue Dolphin. (have)
No. We *aren't having* lunch at the Blue Dolphin. We'*re having* a picnic in the forest. (have)

1 Look. You .... in the sea. (swim)

No. I .... in the sea. I

.... in the swimming pool. (swim)

2 Look. Our French friends ....
badminton on the beach. (play)

No. They .... on the beach. They

.... near the huts. (play)

3 Look. Rebecca .... a photograph.
(take)

No. She .... a photograph. (take)

She .... a new film in the camera.

(put)

4 Look. John .... in the river. (fish)

No. He .... in the river. He

.... in the sea. (fish)

5 Look. We .... out of Sharks
Disco. (come)

No. We .... out of Sharks Disco.

We .... out of the cinema. (come)

6 Look. I .... outside our hut. (sit)

No. You .... outside our hut.

You .... outside the post office.
(sit)

The present continuous tense: questions ▶9.1

5 **a** Study these rules.

Am	I	
		going to Paradise Island?
Is	he she it	having lunch here?
Are	we you they	wearing blue jeans?

> **To make questions with the present continuous, we put 'am' 'is' or 'are' in front of the subject.**
>
> Example
> She is wearing a coat.   *What is she wearing?*
> *Is she wearing a coat?*

b Use these cues. Make questions to complete the dialogues.

Example
What is Terry doing? (What/Terry/do)
He's hiding from three guys.

1 ....?
(Where/Rebecca/go)
She's going to the hospital.

2 ....?
(you/do/your homework)
No, I'm not. I'm listening to the radio.

3 ....?
(Vince and Casey/play/football)
No, they aren't. They're at the cafe.

4 ....?
(What/Kamala/wear)
It's her new coat.

5 ....?
(I/sit/in your seat)
Yes, you are. But it's OK.

6 ....?
(What/Mrs Moore/do)
She's having a driving lesson.

7 ....?
(you/have/a shower)
Yes, I am. What do you want?

Clothes

6 Label the pictures.

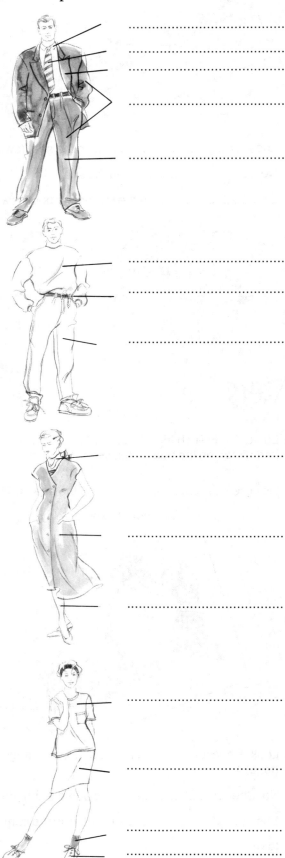

....
....
....
....
....

....
....
....

....

....
....

....
....

....

7 Make true sentences about the people in Exercise 6. Use these cues.

Example
boy/suit *The boy isn't wearing a suit.*

girl/tights ....

man/tie ....

woman/skirt ....

girl/dress ....

boy/jacket ....

woman/scarf ....

man/shirt ....

girl/trousers ....

man/jeans ....

these/those

8 **a** Look.

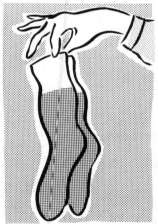
these socks

those socks

b Write 'these' or 'those'.

1 Are ....your socks?

2 A pound of .... apples, please.

3 .... shoes are nice.

4 .... are my holiday photographs.

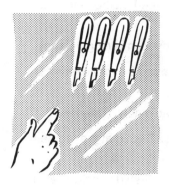

5 How much are .... pens, please?

LISTENING

The present continuous and the present simple ►9.1

9 **a** Study these rules.

We use the present continuous for things that are happening now, at the moment.

Example

*Vince **is getting up**. Vince **is playing** football.*

We use the present simple for things that happen regularly, or every day.

Example
*Vince **gets up** at half past seven every day.*
*Vince **plays** football every Wednesday.*

---

b Write the verb in the correct tense.

1 We .... some English homework every day. (do)

2 Terry .... his English homework at the moment. (do)

3 I .... on a chair now. (sit)

4 Sue .... at half past seven every day. (get up)

5 My parents .... to the shops every Saturday. (go)

6 Kamala .... her teeth at the moment. (clean)

7 I .... my teeth every morning. (clean)

8 Vince .... to the radio every evening. (listen)

9 He .... to the radio now. (listen)

10 I .... jeans and a T-shirt at the moment. (wear)

11 I .... jeans and a T-shirt to school every day. (wear)

10 Look at this letter. Write the verbs in brackets in the correct tense.

Dear Alison,

It's 11 o'clock on Saturday morning and
I .... (sit) in bed.
I .... (wait) for the doctor because I'm
ill. But I'm bored. Kamala .... (help)
in her parents' shop at the moment.
She .... (do) that every Saturday.
Vince isn't here, because he .... (play)
football with Casey today. Mum ....
(shop). She .... (go) to the shops every
Saturday morning. Dad is outside.
He .... (wash) the car. At the moment
I .... (listen) to the radio. The
DJ .... (play) one of my favourite
records. Jason Donovan .... (sing)
'Sealed with a kiss'.

I must go now. The doctor .... (come)
upstairs.
I hope you're well. See you.
        Love, Sue

INTERACTION

Words with no singular

 a Study this rule.

> **Some words in English have got only a plural form:**
>   jeans   tights   trousers   scissors
> **They must take plural articles and verbs.**
>
>   Example
>   *I like **these** jeans. **They're** nice.*

b Complete the dialogues.

Example
Do you like these jeans?
Yes, they're nice.

1 Do you like .... sweater?

   Yes, ... nice.

2 How much .... trousers?

   .... £21.

3 How much .... dress?

   .... £19.

   Can I try .... on?

4 Can I have .... belt, please?

   Yes. Do you want .... in a bag?

   No, thank you. I can put .... in this bag.

5 Can I have .... scissors, please?

   Yes. Do you want .... in a bag?

   No, thank you. I can put .... in this bag.

6 Look at .... tights. Do you like

   ....?

   Mm, yes, and .... cheap, too.

7 Look at .... shirt. Do you like

   ....?

   Mm, yes, and .... cheap, too.

PROJECT

Short forms

▼13 **Write these sentences with the short forms of the verbs.**

1 Casey does not play the guitar.

....

2 I am wearing my new jeans.

....

3 She has not got the photographs.

....

4 We do not go to school on Saturdays.

....

5 I cannot go to the party.

....

6 It is ten o'clock.

....

7 We are going to the disco.

....

8 I have got a new tie.

....

W	O	R	D	C	H	A	I	N

▼14 **How many names of clothes can you find in the wordchain? Circle them.**

trouser(s)kirt(e)inmsunglassesposhirtiegbwoiuiightshoesocksseeprkertsweaterdessskliatrackswitessuitwjekjjumperkickjacketbeltshortsewheadbandeltrainersoc

Paragraphs

▼15 **Write the sentences in the correct order to make paragraphs.**

a
John's wearing brown shorts and a white T-shirt.
John's also wearing black trainers, white socks and a red baseball cap.
The shorts are £25 from Your Thing and the T-shirt is £11.50 from Fashion Warehouse.
The cap is £10 from Allsports.
Here's something for the summer.

....
....
....
....
....
....
....
....
....

b
Her dress is £52.50 from Nikos and her shoes are £25 from Dolcis.
The bag is £28 from The Bag Shop.
She's wearing a short pink dress with red stockings and black shoes.
Is Ann going to a party?
Ann's also wearing long earrings and she's carrying a red bag.
It also comes in yellow and green.

....
....
....
....
....
....
....
....

School uniform

Most schools in Britain have a school uniform and pupils must wear it. Different schools have different colours, but here is a typical uniform.

Pupils in the sixth form (aged 17 and 18) don't usually wear uniforms.

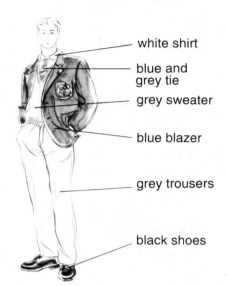

white shirt
blue and grey tie
grey sweater
blue blazer
grey trousers
black shoes

white blouse
blue and grey tie
grey sweater
blue blazer
blue skirt
blue socks
black shoes
blue and white dress

COMPARISON

....
....
....
....
....

Compare this to your country.
• Do you wear a uniform?
• What do you wear to school?

Self-check

1 Complete the dialogues.

1 What .... doing?

We .... lunch. (have)

2 Is Vince in his bedroom?

Yes. He .... the guitar. (practise)

3 Look. There's our new neighbour. She

.... at that table over there. (sit)

4 What .... Sue and Kamala

.... at the moment? (do)

They .... anything. (not do)

5 Listen. That's Casey.

What .... ? (do)

2 Write the verb in brackets in the correct tense.

1 I .... football on TV every Saturday. (watch)

2 I .... a great match at the moment. (watch)

3 Vince .... a blue sweater today. (wear)

4 Sue .... to the hospital every Wednesday. (go)

5 Kamala .... in the shop after school every day. (help)

6 She .... in the shop today, because she's late. (not help)

3 Complete these dialogues.

1 How much .... trousers?

.... £15.

Can I try .... on?

Of course.

2 How much .... T-shirt?

.... £5.

I'll take ....

3 Do you like .... jeans?

Yes, ... very nice.

Check your answers with a partner. If there is anything you do not understand, ask your teacher or check in the Grammar reference section on pages 109–114 of your Student's Book.

67

Revision crossword

[crossword grid]

Clues

ACROSS

3 That's my new boyfriend. What's ___ name?
5 It's ___ right.
6 post ___
7 Manchester United is a football ___ .
10 This big fish eats people.
12 You buy food here.

15

17 Jason Donovan is a pop ___ .
18 Where ___ you going?

21

22 What's ___ address?
23 The opposite of dark hair is ___ hair.
28 You cut things with these.
30 How much are ___ badges over there?
37 We aren't doing ___ at the moment.
39 not the same

DOWN

1 What time ___ Terry come home?
2 There are lots ___ things to do here.
3 Can I ___ you?
4 School ___ at 9 o'clock.
5 Are you from Spain?
  Yes, I ___ .
8 What's the ___?
9 an ice ___

10

11 Where's Casey?
  ___'s upstairs.
12 You buy this on holiday.
13 I haven't got ___ money.
14 You eat this in the morning.
16 the opposite of 'late'
17 You can swim or fish here.

19

20 You do this with your eyes.
24 ___ this your pen?
25 Where ___ you live?
26 We're going to the cinema. Do you want to join ___?
27 What are you ___?
29 I ___ in bed late on Sundays.

31

  It's ___ past ten.
32 I need ___ new clothes.
33 the opposite of 'good'
34 ___, two, three

35

36 Where's Terry? I can't see ___ .
38 Let's go ___ the cinema.

VICTORIA ROAD

On my way

1 **a Look.**

I'm on **my** way **to** the shops.

She's on **her** way **back from** the shops.

b Where are the people on their way to or back from? Complete the following sentences.

They're on .... way .... school.

We're ....
from ....

Mr Smith's ....

He ....

We ....
....

They ....

In the park

2 Yesterday there was a robbery in the park. Look at the picture. Label it. Use these words.

lake	boat	bag	table	bench
grass	waiter	bridge	chair	girl
boy	man	woman	dog	bird

The verb 'to be': past tense ▶11.1

3 **a** **Study these rules.**

I		
He	was	
She	was not	
It	wasn't	in the park.
		at the cafe.
We	were	near the lake.
You	were not	
They	weren't	

'was' and 'were' have no short form.
'wasn't' and 'weren't' are the short forms of
'was not' and 'were not'.

b These people were in the park yesterday.
Complete what they say.

1 I .... on the bridge.

2 We .... in a boat. The boat
.... under the bridge.

3 We .... near the lake. Our dogs
.... in the water.

4 I .... on the grass.

5 We .... on the bench.

6 I .... at the cafe.

7 I .... at the cafe. My coat
.... on the chair and my bag
.... on the table.

c The boy and girl by the lake are talking about the robbery. The boy has got a lot of information wrong. Correct what he says.

Example
There were four people at the cafe.
No. There weren't four people at the cafe. There were two people.

1 The man and woman were on the bridge.

No. They ....

....

2 There were three girls in the boat.

No. There ....

....

3 The woman's bag was under the table.

No. It ....

....

4 The boy's hair was dark.

No. It ....

....

5 We were on the grass.

No. We ....

....

The verb 'to be': past tense questions ▶11.1

4 a Study these rules.

Was	I he she it	in the park?
		at the cafe?
Were	we you they	near the lake?

> To make questions in the past tense of 'to be' we put 'was' or 'were' in front of the subject.
>
> Example
> **They were** at the cafe.
> **Were they** at the cafe?
> Where **were they?**

b A policeman is talking to the girl near the lake. Use these cues. Make the policeman's questions.

1 ....?
(Where/you)
I was near the lake.

2 ....?
(You/alone)
No, I was with my boyfriend, my little sister and our two dogs.

3 ....?
(your boyfriend/near the lake, too)
Yes, he was.

4 ....?
(Where/your little sister)
She was on the bridge.

5 ....?
(your dogs/with her)
No, they weren't. They were in the water.

6 ....?
(How many people/there/at the cafe)
There were two people – the waiter and a woman.

7 ....?
(Where/the woman's bag)
It was on the table.

5 Complete this conversation with 'was', 'wasn't', 'were' or 'weren't'.

A .... you at the match last night?

B Yes, I ....

A .... it a good match?

B It .... all right.

A What about Gascoigne? .... he good?

B Oh yes. He .... brilliant. But the others .... very good. Barnes .... terrible. Why .... you there?

A I .... at the New Kids on the Block concert.

B Oh .... they good?

A They .... great.

B Where .... the concert?

A It .... at the Albert Hall.

READING

The past simple tense: regular verbs ►11.2

 a Study these rules.

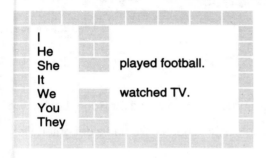

present
I **play** tennis every day.
He **watches** TV every day.

past
I **played** tennis yesterday.
He **watched** TV yesterday

To make the past tense, we add -ed to the verb stem.
The past tense is the same for all persons.

I
He
She
It   played football.
We
You watched TV.
They

Note the spelling rules.

When the verb ends in -e, we just add -d.

Example
chase
The three boys chased Terry.

When the verb ends in a consonant + -y, we drop the -y and add -ied.

Example
carry
Kamala carried Sue's coat and bags.

When the verb has a short vowel and one consonant, we double the consonant and add -ed.

Example
stop
I stopped and looked at the monster.

Casey's weekend

b Complete what Casey says. Use the verbs below. You can use 'be' more than once.

stay	move	want	walk	try
listen	miss	help	start	arrive
rain	watch	wait	carry	be
play	finish			

On Saturday morning I .... football with the school team. In the afternoon Sue and I .... old Mr Kelly at number 12. He can't walk upstairs any more. So we .... some things downstairs for him. We .... his bed downstairs. We .... to move his wardrobe, too, but it .... too heavy.

There .... a good film at the cinema this weekend. We .... to catch the 6.30 bus. We .... for Terry, but he .... late, (as usual), and we .... the bus. So we ...., but when we .... on our way into town, it .... to rain. When we ...., we .... very wet. But it .... a good film.

On Sunday it .... again. So I .... at home. I .... a video and .... to the radio. In the evening I .... my homework.

Years

 a Look.

We write	We say
1492	fourteen ninety-two.
1904	nineteen oh four

b How do we say these?

1625 ....

1992 ....

1807 ....

1516 ....

1763 ....

2190 ....

73

LISTENING

Time

▼8 **Match these words to the correct thing.**

an hour	a year	a day
a minute	a week	half an hour

ago

▼9 a **Look.**

She wasn't at the hospital **half an hour ago**.
Lucy Loxley died **a long time ago**.

b **Complete these.**

Example
The robbery happened at 10 o'clock.
It's now 12 o'clock.
The robbery happened two hours ago.

1 School started at 9 o'clock. It's now 9.25.

   School started ....

2 We moved to this house in 1989. It's now 1991.

   We moved to ....

3 We arrived on Monday. It's now Wednesday.

   We ....

4 My grandfather died in 1970. It's now 1991.

   My ....

5 Your appointment was at 2 o'clock. It's 3 o'clock now.

   Your appointment was ....

The Grey Lady

▼10 **Complete the story.**

A long time ago a man called Sir Roger Loxley

.... this house. He had a daughter. Her

name .... Lucy.

Sir Roger .... and he always

.... money. A rich neighbour, Lord

Griston, ... to marry Lucy. He

.... old and ugly, but he .... Sir

Roger a lot of money.

Sir Roger .... Lord Griston's money, but

Lucy .... to marry him. She ....

to marry Thomas Mowbray. Thomas ....

in the village. He .... young and

handsome and he .... Lucy, but he was

poor.

When Lucy .... to marry Lord Griston, Sir

Roger .... her in her room. Lucy

.... and .... One night she

.... out of a window and ....

Today some people see Lucy's ghost in this room.

People call her the Grey Lady.

INTERACTION

Male and female

11 Fill in the missing words.

....	woman
prince	....
....	queen
....	waitress
boy	....
policeman	....
....	mother
....	sister
....	girlfriend
son	....
lord	....

You'd better

12 Complete the speech bubbles. Use these words.

call the doctor   go   get a taxi   hide
call the police   get up   have a rest
go to the dentist

1
You ....
....

2
The bus is late. We ....
....

3
It's the police. You ....

4
We ....

5
I ....

6
You ....

7
I ....

8
We ....

Using notes

13 **a** Look at the notes and the paragraph. In the paragraph underline the additional words.

> **Giant statues**
> Easter Island, Pacific Ocean
> over 600 statues, 1–20 metres tall
> made from volcanic rock
> 1000–400 years ago
>
> **Mystery**
> Why did they make the statues?
> Statues of real people? } We don't know.
> How did they move them?

On Easter Island in the Pacific Ocean there are over 600 giant statues. They are between 1 and 20 metres tall. The people on the island made them from volcanic rock between 1000 and 400 years ago. The statues are a mystery. Why did the people make the statues? Are they statues of real people? How did they move the statues? We don't know the answers to these questions.

b Write a paragraph from these notes.

> **Stonehenge, Wiltshire, England**
> giant circle of stones
> nearly 80 stones, 2–9 metres high
> stones from different parts of Britain
> 5000–3500 years ago
>
> **Mystery**
> Why did people build it?
> Why stones from other parts of Britain? } We don't know.
> How did they transport them?

....
....
....
....
....
....
....
....
....
....

Monsters and ghosts

There are a lot of old houses and castles in Britain. People often believe that there are ghosts in these buildings. The ghosts are always someone who died there a long time ago.

There are also stories about monsters. The most famous monster is the Loch Ness Monster (or Nessie).

Loch Ness is in Scotland. It is very deep and the water is very dark. People see strange things there and a lot of people believe that a kind of dinosaur still lives there.

On Dartmoor, in south-west England, some people have seen a very large black cat – as big as a lion. They call it the Beast of Dartmoor.

COMPARISON

- Are there any stories like this in your country?
- What famous 'ghosts' and 'monsters' are there?

LEARNING DIARY

Self-check

1 Complete this story.

Use these verbs. Some are used more than once.

open	want	jump	disappear	live
appear	pick up	close	carry	
stop	be	walk	look	

In 1989 I .... near the sea. One night I

.... on my way home in my car. It

.... a dark night. Suddenly something

.... on the beach. It .... a

spaceship. It .... very big. I ....

the car and .... at it. After about five

minutes a door .... and some men

.... There .... three of them.

They .... small and red. They

.... out of the spaceship and

.... along the beach. I .... to

take a photograph, but my camera .... in

the car. Near the beach there .... five or

six cars. The three spacemen .... one of

the cars. They .... it into the spaceship.

The door .... and the spaceship

....

2 A policeman is asking the man some questions. Use these cues. Make the questions.

1 .... ?
(Why/you/near the beach)
I was on my way home.

2 .... ?
(Where/the spaceship)
It was on the beach.

3 .... ?
(How many men/there)
There were three of them.

4 .... ?
(they/big)
No, they weren't. They were small.

5 .... ?
(What colour/they)
They were red.

3 Complete these sentences to make true sentences about the story.

1 The spaceship .... in a park. It
.... on the beach.

2 It .... a small spaceship. It
.... very big.

3 There .... five spacemen. There
.... three of them.

4 The spacemen .... blue. They
.... red.

5 They .... big. They ....
small.

Check your answers with a partner. If there is anything you do not understand, ask your teacher or check in the Grammar reference section on pages 109–114 of your Student's Book.

VICTORIA ROAD
Useful expressions

1 Complete the dialogue with the following.

Don't do that!   There it is!   Oh dear!
What's going on?   you'd better   rat
It's all my fault   something strange
You'd better go to the hospital

1

There's ....
over there. What is it?

Oh, that's my pet ....

2

No. ....

....
It's escaping.

3

....

4

....

Ow. My hand!

5

....

Oh, I'm sorry. ....

6

And ....

catch that rat.

78

The past simple tense: irregular verbs ►12.1

2 a Study these rules.

I		
He		
She		went to London.
It		
We		escaped.
You		
They		

Some verbs have a regular past tense.

Example
jump   *jumped*
move   *moved*
carry   *carried*

Some verbs have an irregular past tense.

Example
see   *saw*
go   *went*
take   *took*

The past tense is the same for all persons.

Kamala's day

b Complete the sentences with the verb in brackets.

This is what happened to Kamala yesterday.

1 She .... school with Sue at 3.20. (leave)

2 Sue .... to the cinema with two other girls. (go)

3 Kamala .... Sue's coat and bags. (take)

4 She .... the bus. (miss)

5 At Victoria Road she .... Terry. (see)

6 She .... Sue's coat and bags to Terry. (give)

7 She was in a hurry. So she .... to her parents' shop. (run)

8 She .... her tea. (have)

9 She .... in the shop. (help)

10 She .... her homework. (do)

11 A police car .... outside the shop. (stop)

12 Vince, Casey and a policewoman .... into the shop. (come)

Your day

3 What did you do yesterday? Write eight sentences to describe your day.

....

....

....

....

....

....

....

....

LANGUAGE WORK

The missing film star

4 Complete the story. Use the verbs below.

arrive	wait	get	find	disappear
go	say	cannot	have	call
leave	give	see	take	come (× 2)

Film star disappears

Two days ago the famous film star, Jennifer O'Neill, ... She .... home at 10 o'clock on Wednesday morning and she .... to the station. Her neighbour .... her outside her house.

'A taxi .... at 10 o'clock. Jennifer .... out of her house. She .... "hello" to me and then she .... into the taxi. She .... a small bag.' The taxi .... her to the station.

When Jennifer's husband, Robert, ... home in the evening he .... find Jennifer. He .... till 10 o'clock. Then he............. the police.

Yesterday a man .... Jennifer's bag at Dover station. He .... it to the police.

The past simple tense: negative ►12.2

5 a Study these rules.

| I He She It We You They | did not didn't | go to work have lunch stay at home miss the bus | yesterday. last week. |

To make the past simple negative we put 'didn't' in front of the verb stem.
'didn't' is the short form of 'did not'.
'didn't' shows the past tense. So the verb is in the infinitive form.

Example
I went **positive**
but
I didn't **go** **negative**

b Here are some statements about the Jennifer O'Neill story, but they are all wrong. Correct them.

Example
Jennifer O'Neill disappeared three days ago.
She didn't disappear three days ago. She disappeared two days ago.

1 She left home at 11 o'clock.

....
....

2 She went to the airport.

....
....

3 Her brother saw her at 10 o'clock.

....
....

4 A taxi arrived at 11 o'clock.

....
....

5 She had two large bags.

....
....

6 Her neighbour called the police.

....
....

7 Her husband came home in the afternoon.

....
....

8 A man found her bag in London.

....
....

9 The man threw the bag away.

....
....

Your day

6 Did you do any of these things yesterday? Write true sentences.

Example
I stayed at home.
or
I didn't stay at home.

stay at home	buy a car
throw your friend in a lake	miss a bus
go to an airport	run ten kilometres
take some photographs	find a bag of money
see a famous person	rob a bank
have lunch with the Queen	

....
....
....
....
....
....
....
....
....

READING

A crossword

7 Complete the crossword.

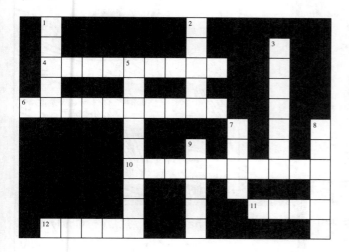

Clues

ACROSS

4

6

10

11

12 This is short for 'aeroplane'.

DOWN

1 ___ attack

2

3 Planes land here.
5 You wear this when you jump out of an aeroplane.
7 This is white.

8

9 This person flies a plane.

Cindy and the Golden Cat of Caldor

8 Complete this story. Use the past tense of these verbs. Some are used more than once.

hit	grab	throw	fly	land
throw	run	put	leave	go
take	jump	give	be	catch
attack	escape	swim	climb	can

This is the Golden Cat of Caldor. The evil Doctor Strange wants the cat. You must take it to the Secretary General of the United Nations in New York.

1 Lord Good .... the Golden Cat of Caldor to Cindy.

2 Cindy .... the cat and ....
her old friend. She .... into the street.

3 But Doctor Strange and his men ....
her. They .... Cindy and
.... her into a bag.

81

4 They .... the bag to the airport and
.... it into a helicopter.

5 When they .... near Doctor Strange's
secret island, Cindy .... from the bag.
She .... out of the helicopter and
.... in the sea.

6 Three large sharks .... Cindy. She
.... them and they .... away.

7 Cindy .... to a small island. She
.... a tree. From the top of the tree she
.... see the airport on Doctor Strange's
island. The helicopter .... at the airport.

8 At that moment a small plane .... over
Cindy. She .... up and .... the wheels.

9 When the plane .... , Cindy ....
to the helicopter. The Golden Cat ....
on one of the seats in the helicopter.

10 Cindy .... the pilot out of the helicopter.

11 Cindy .... to New York. She
.... the cat to the Secretary
General of the United Nations

82

LISTENING

Prepositions of place: in/at/to/on ▶12.3

a Study these rules.

> **We use 'to' when there is movement.**
>
>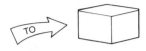
>
> Example
> *I'm going to France.*
> *Kamala gave the coat to Terry.*
>
> **Note: We say 'arrive at'**
>
> **We use 'into' and 'out of' when there is movement.**
>
>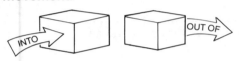
>
> Example
> *They threw Cindy into the helicopter.*
> *Cindy jumped out of the helicopter.*
>
> **We usually use 'in' when there is no movement.**
> **We use 'in' for rooms, cars, streets, towns,**
> **countries and newspapers/magazines.**
>
> Example
> *He's in the kitchen.*
> *There were three men in the car.*
> *We're staying in New York.*
> *I read it in the newspaper.*
>
> **We use 'at' when there is no movement. We**
> **use 'at' for buildings and similar places.**
>
> Example
> *She's at the shops.*
> *We're at school.*
>
> **We can use 'on' with or without movement.**
>
> Example
> *There's a book on the table.*
> *Put the books on the table.*
>
> **We also use 'on' for TV and radio programmes,**
> **buses, trains, ships and planes.**
>
> Example
> *It was on the news.*
> *Terry met Kamala on the bus.*
>
> **Note: You get into and out of a car. You get on**
> **and off a bus, train, plane, ship, motorbike,**
> **bicycle or horse.**

b Put in the correct prepositions.

1 There was a robbery .... London today.

2 It was .... the bank in Fenmore Street.

3 At ten o'clock three men arrived .... the bank .... a blue car.

4 Two of the men got .... the car and went .... the bank. One stayed .... the car.

5 The police arrested all the men and took them .... the police station.

6 A photograph of the robbers was .... the newspapers and they were .... the TV too.

Trouble for Terry

10 Complete these sentences with the correct preposition.

1 .... (On/In) Wednesdays Sue goes .... (to/at) the hospital .... (after/at) school. But she wasn't .... (to/at) the hospital today. She went .... (to/in) the cinema .... (with/of) some friends.

2 Vince and Casey were .... (in/on) the park. They were on their way back .... (to/from) football. They found Sue's books .... (at/on) the grass. Her bag was .... (in/under) a bench and her coat was .... (in/on) the lake. But Sue wasn't there. And she wasn't .... (to/at) home.

3 Terry met Kamala when they got .... (off/of) the bus. .... (At/In) the corner .... (off/of) Victoria Road they saw Tooley and his friends sitting .... (on/at) a wall. Kamala gave Sue's coat and bags .... (to/of) Terry. Then she went .... (to/at) the shop.

4 Sue got back .... (to/from) the cinema .... (to/at) half past six. She went .... (to/from) Kamala's place. Vince, Casey and Kamala were there .... (with/at) a policewoman. Kamala told them .... (to/about) the three boys. Then Terry appeared .... (at/to) the window.

INTERACTION

The past simple tense: questions ►12.2

 a Study these rules.

Did	I he she it we you they	go to the Live Aid concert? see the news? help the people of Africa?

To make questions in the past simple tense we use 'did' + subject + infinitive.

Examples
*She **went** to London.*
***Did** she **go** to London?*
*Where **did** she **go**?*

We use the infinitive of the verb NOT the past tense.
We use 'did' for all persons.

---

b Jennifer O'Neill returned yesterday after five days. Some reporters are interviewing her. Here are some cues from a reporter's notebook. Make the questions.

Example
Where/go   *Where did you go?*
leave/England   *Did you leave England?*

How/travel .... ?

What clothes/take .... ?

Where/stay .... ?

see/the news .... ?

When/come home .... ?

What/do .... ?

How/get money .... ?

someone/find .... ?

Why/disappear .... ?

12 Make the questions to complete this conversation. Use the cues.

Example
(have a good holiday)
Did you have a good holiday?
Oh yes, it was great.

1 (Where/go)

.... ?
We went to France.

2 (Who/go with)

.... ?
I went with my parents.

3 (fly)

.... ?
No, we went by car.

4 (stay in a hotel)

.... ?
No, we didn't. We took our caravan.

5 (visit Paris)

.... ?
Oh yes, we did.

6 (like Paris)

.... ?
Oh, yes. It was wonderful.

7 (What/see)

.... ?
We saw lots of things. You know, the Eiffel Tower, the Louvre Museum.

8 (buy any souvenirs)

.... ?
Oh yes. I bought lots of things.

9 (get back yesterday)

.... ?
No, we came back on Saturday.

PROJECT

 a Find 20 more irregular past tenses in the verbsquare.

S	L	A	S	Y	D	F	L	E	W	B	S	O	N
Z	W	C	R	C	A	K	B	R	O	U	G	H	T
B	C	A	U	G	H	T	O	J	K	M	K	N	R
Q	H	P	M	G	N	T	I	M	E	J	S	A	W
X	T	F	O	U	N	D	M	C	U	L	L	I	Q
Y	F	E	U	E	X	L	P	Q	P	T	O	O	K
F	S	W	W	H	T	D	L	E	F	T	Z	D	A
B	A	Z	K	D	E	H	E	K	Y	G	M	I	N
C	I	F	O	M	P	X	R	P	S	M	J	D	H
W	D	A	A	W	H	T	Z	E	R	A	Q	F	R
J	V	C	V	I	G	A	V	E	W	D	G	E	U
B	E	R	D	I	X	S	H	W	T	E	F	L	T
B	D	A	U	Y	B	H	A	C	C	O	U	L	D
C	V	N	C	A	M	E	D	E	U	A	O	G	V

b Write the verbs in this chart, together with their infinitives.

infinitive	past
say	*said*

Linking sentences

 **a** Look.

> The plane landed.
> Cindy ran to the helicopter.
> She threw the pilot out.

We can join these sentences like this.

> When the plane landed, Cindy ran to the helicopter and threw the pilot out.

b Join these sentences in the same way.

1 Lord Good gave Cindy the cat.
Cindy said goodbye.
She left her old friend.

....

....

2 Doctor Strange's men saw Cindy.
They grabbed her.
They put her into a bag.

....

....

3 Cindy escaped from the bag.
She jumped out of the helicopter.
She landed in the sea.

....

....

....

4 Cindy swam to a small island.
She climbed a tree.
She saw Doctor Strange's island.

....

....

5 A small plane flew over Cindy.
She jumped up.
She grabbed the wheels.

....

....

6 Cindy arrived in New York.
She went to the United Nations.
She gave the cat to the Secretary General.

....

....

....

15 How many past tenses can you find in the wordchain? Circle them.

wasawoputookrawentadid...
...diedodleftherewantedarspicamea...
brought couldolmaderskflewalked said...
...disankeimtrugavelgotetahibl...
...ewytewerecriedunfyustoppedint...

Newspaper headlines

16 Look at the newspaper articles. Choose the correct headlines. Draw lines to connect the headlines to the articles.

1 **Arsenal are champions**
2 **Girl escapes from M6 accident**
3 **United win again**
4 **£1 million robbery**
5 **Big prize win**
6 **Woman dies in car crash**
7 **Smile. You're on TV.**

a | There was a serious accident on the M6 near Birmingham yesterday afternoon. A green Ford Escort ran into the back of a lorry. The driver of the car, Mrs Jane Wilkins, 32, died.

b | Thieves broke into an electrical shop last night and stole videos and televisions worth over £300,000. However, the shop's own security cameras recorded the robbery. Later the police arrested two men.

c | At first he didn't believe it, but yesterday was Colin Greene's lucky day. He won over £1 million in a lottery. Colin is now planning a round-the-world holiday for his family.

d | It wasn't an easy game, but once again the boys from Manchester showed why they are the champions. United's 1–0 victory over Arsenal keeps them at the top of the table. The goal came after fifty minutes from

CULTURE SPOT

The news

You can listen to the news on the radio, watch it on TV or read it in the newspapers.

Most radio programmes give the news every hour.

On TV there are three main news programmes. In the morning there is breakfast time television from 7 o'clock to 9 o'clock. The early evening news is at 6 o'clock, when people get home from work. The main news programme is at 9 or 10 o'clock in the evening.

COMPARISON

Compare this to your country.
- When are news programmes on the TV and the radio?
- Do you watch the news?

86

LEARNING DIARY

Self-check

1 Complete this story with the past tense of these verbs. Some are used more than once.

shout   throw   stop   escape   say
get   find   go   bring   crash
can   cry   not be have   see
come   look   be   run   leave
cannot   happen   die

BABY ESCAPES FROM PLANE CRASH

A baby, Sabina Lori, ... from a plane

crash yesterday. The DC10 .... near the

airport at Sioux City, Iowa. It .... at

four o'clock in the afternoon. The crash

.... baby Sabina out of the plane and a

stewardess .... her. The baby's father, Mr

Lori, ..., 'When the plane .... ,

I .... see a light. I .... out of my

seat and I .... away from the plane. I

.... my wife, but Sabina ....

with her.'

The plane .... on fire, but Mr Lori

.... his wife and .... back into

the plane. He .... for Sabina, but he

.... find her.

'When I .... out of the plane again, I

.... a woman. She .... a baby

in her arms. I .... and the woman

.... the baby to me. It ....

Sabina and she .... alive. I just

.... 178 people .... from the

plane crash, but 115 other people ....'

2 Here are some facts about the crash, but they are incorrect. Write them correctly.

Example
The crash threw Mr Lori out of the plane.
The crash didn't throw Mr Lori out of the plane. It threw Sabina out of the plane.

1 The pilot found Sabina.

....

....

....

2 The crash happened in the evening.

....

....

....

3 Mr Lori stayed with his wife.

....

....

....

4 He saw a man with a baby.

....

....

....

3 A reporter is asking Mr Lori questions. Use these cues. Make the questions.

1 (What time/the crash/happen)

.... ?

2 (Where/the plane/crash)

.... ?

3 (all the people/escape)

.... ?

4 (you/find Sabina)

.... ?

5 (How/you escape)

.... ?

6 (you/find/your wife)

.... ?

Check your answers with a partner. If there is anything you do not understand, ask your teacher or check in the Grammar reference section on pages 109–114 of your Student's Book.

UNIT 13 The movies

VICTORIA ROAD
Prepositions

1 **a** Label the diagrams with the words below.

in   out   away   up   round   on   off   down

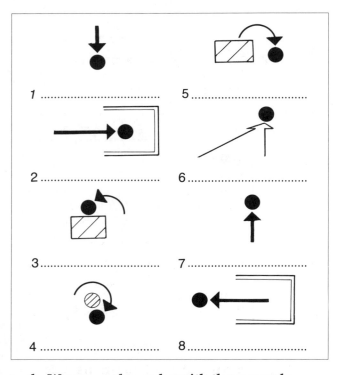

1 ....   5 ....

2 ....   6 ....

3 ....   7 ....

4 ....   8 ....

b We can make verbs with these words.

Example
run away   *fly away*   *swim away*
go out   *come out*   *keep out*

c Complete these with one of the words in a.

1 Put your hands ....
and don't turn ....

I'm sorry. It just came ....

2

3 Please come ....
and sit ....

4 Why are you putting your coat
.... ?

I'm going ....

5 Fill it .... , please.

6 Put your gun ....
and come ....
with your hands up.

7 Wake ....

8 Look. They're running ....

88

LANGUAGE WORK

Adverbs ►13.1

2 **a** **Look.**

He's singing **loudly**.

Adverbs tell us how someone does something. We put an adverb after the verb.

b **Complete these sentences with these words.**

quietly   hard   fast   loudly   carefully

1 She's running very ....

2 He's walking ....

3 They're working ....

4 He's playing the guitar ....

5 She's talking ....

Adjectives and adverbs ►13.1

3 **a** **Study these rules.**

Adjectives describe a noun. They say what something is like.

Example
*Cindy is a **brave** girl.*

Adverbs describe the verb. They say how someone does something.

Example
*Cindy fights **bravely**.*

Most adverbs end in -ly.

Example
adjective brave
adverb *bravely*

These adverbs are irregular.

adjective	adverb
fast	fast
hard	hard
friendly	friendly
good	well

b Look at the list of adverbs and adjectives. First check any new words in your dictionary.

weakly	easy	brave	hard	sad
new	hardly	easily	newly	quick
heavy	fast	quickly	friendly	bravely
big	strong	sadly	regularly	weak
regular	heavily			

c Complete the letter. Choose the correct words from the list above. Some are used more than once.

Dear Charles Atlas

Last summer I went to the beach with my ....
girlfriend, Tracy. A .... guy was there. He wasn't
very .... He kicked sand in my face and
pushed me .... I fought ...., but it was an
.... fight for him. He was very .... and I
was very .... He laughed at me and I walked
away .... Then I read your advertisement. I
bought your book and I practised ....
Soon I became .... I could run .... and
I could lift .... things ....

Last week, I went back to the beach. This time the
guy wasn't so .... When he saw my ....
muscles, he ran away ....

Thank you.

Yours sincerely

John Smith

Ordinal numbers

 a Study these rules.

> **To make ordinal numbers we add -th to the number.**
>
> Example
> four   *fourth*
> nineteen   *nineteenth*
>
> **These ordinals are irregular.**
>
> | | ordinals |
> |-------|----------|
> | one | first |
> | two | second |
> | three | third |
>
> **These ordinals have an irregular spelling.**
>
> | | ordinals |
> |--------|----------|
> | five | fifth |
> | eight | eighth |
> | nine | ninth |
> | twelve | twelfth |
> | twenty | twentieth |
>
> **We can write ordinal numbers in a short form. We use the number and the last two letters of the word.**
>
> Example
> first   *1st*
> twenty-second   *22nd*
> sixth   *6th*

b Write these numbers in full.

31st ....

16th ....

12th ....

3rd ....

29th ....

62nd ....

50th ....

8th ....

Where do they live?

▼5 Which floor do they live on?

Example
Carol and Bill Black live on the first floor.

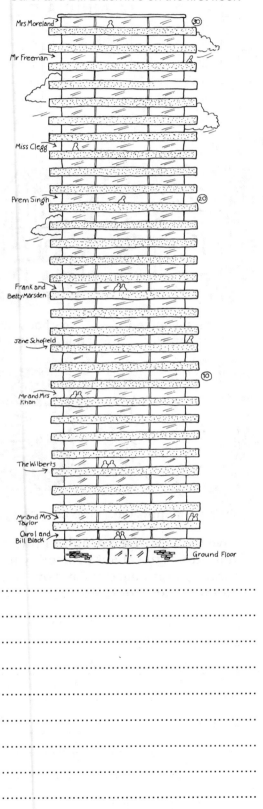

....
....
....
....
....
....
....
....
....
....
....

enough

▼6 **a** Look.

He was **good enough** to win the Mr Universe competition.

b Complete these dialogues. Use these words.

long	tall	old	loud	fast
short	big	heavy	good	

1
I'm sorry. You aren't ....
.... to buy a drink.

2
It isn't ....

3
It isn't ....

91

4

I can't hear it. It isn't ....

5

This is terrible, Sarah. It isn't
....

6

Oh dear! I'm not ....

7

Is that .... ?

8

I'm afraid you aren't ....

9

No. You weren't ....

7 Complete the crossword with the months of the year.

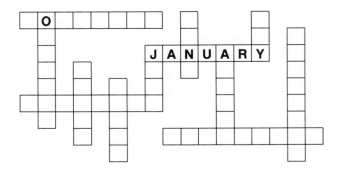

8 **a** Look.

He's **seventeen years old.**

This house is **five hundred years old.**

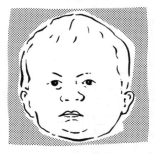

She's **six months old.**

This car's **one year old.**

b Give the ages of ten people or things in your life. Write about yourself, your parents, your house or flat, your car, brothers and sisters, etc.

I'm ....

My ....

My ....

Our ....

Our car ....

....

....

....

....

....

LISTENING

Dates ▶13.2

 a Study these rules.

We write	We say
12 February or 12th February	the twelfth of February

We write months with a capital letter.

b Complete the table.

We write	We say
1 September	....
20 August	....
22 July	....
8 January	....
25 December	....
11 March	....
6 May	....
17 April	....
Add your birthday	
....	....

Prepositions of time: in, at, on

 a Study these rules.

We use 'in' for years, months and parts of the day.

Example
in July
in 1930
in August 1970
in the evening (But note: at night)

We use 'at' for times of the day.

Example
at half past three
at 10.15

We use 'on' for days and dates.

Example
on Thursday
on 9 August
on Thursday 9 August 1990

b Write the correct preposition.

1	 1989	10	...... July 1986
2	.... Tuesday	11	...... the afternoon
3	.... 30 February	12	 1942
4	.... 8.15	13	...... Saturday
5	.... November	14	...... the morning
6	.... night	15	...... half past seven
7	.... April	16	...... quarter to three
8	.... Wednesday 19 May		
9	.... Friday 11 November 1948		

11 a Complete these sentences with the correct times: time, day, date, month or year.

1 I was born ....

2 I get up ....

3 The Second World War started ....
....

4 We have English ....

5 My mother's birthday is ....
....

6 Our summer holidays start ....
....

7 Last year I went on holiday ....
....

8 The last Olympic Games were ....
....

9 I go to bed ....

10 We don't go to school ....
....

b Make a list of six important dates in your year, e.g. birthdays in your family, holidays etc.

....
....
....
....
....
....

INTERACTION

12 Write the questions.

Example
Come on. The plane leaves soon.
What time does it leave?

1 Come on. The bus goes soon.

.... ?

2 Come on. The film starts soon.

.... ?

3 Come on. The shop closes soon.

.... ?

4 Come on. The programme finishes soon.

.... ?

5 Come on. The match starts soon.

.... ?

6 Come on. The plane arrives soon.

.... ?

13 Complete the dialogues with the missing questions.

Let's go to the movies on Friday.

OK. .... ?
Brooklyn Girl.

.... ?
Woody Allen and Diane Keaton

.... ?
It's on at the Classic.

.... ?
4.15 and 7 o'clock.

PROJECT

Spelling 'ie' or 'ei'

14 Complete these words.

rec____ve   fr____ndly   interv____w

qu____tly   bel____ve   mov____s

twent____th   n____ghbour   carr____d

hurr____s   p____ce   sc____nce

____ght   ____ghteen

Describing a film

15 a Read this.

Last week I went to the cinema. I saw Cindy and the Golden Cat. It starred Linda Twine as Cindy and Michael Orlof as the evil Doctor Strange.

Doctor Strange wanted the Golden Cat. When the film started, Lord Good, Cindy's friend, gave the Golden Cat to Cindy. 'Take this to the Secretary General of the United Nations!' he said. But Doctor Strange and his men caught Cindy. They put her in a bag and threw the bag into the helicopter. Cindy escaped and found Doctor Strange's secret island. She got the Golden Cat again and flew to New York. At the end she gave the Golden Cat to the Secretary General of the United Nations.

I liked the film. It was very exciting.

b Describe a film that you have seen recently. Answer these questions.

What was the film called?
Who was in it?
What happened?
What was the film like?

Use the text above as a model.

....

....

....

....

....

....

....

....

....

....

....

....

....

....

Going to the movies

Most towns in Britain have one cinema. Cinemas often have three parts or studios. They usually show a new film each week.

Cinemas are quite expensive in Britain. It costs about £5 to get in.

Many people watch films at home on video. You can rent videos for about £2 a night. There are a lot of video libraries in towns. You can often rent videos from petrol stations and newsagents' shops too.

COMPARISON

Compare this to your country.
- Do people usually watch films at the cinema or on video?
- Are cinemas expensive?
- Can you rent videos in your town?
- How often do you go to the cinema or watch a video?

LEARNING DIARY

Self-check

1 Look at the alphabet. Complete the sentences.

a b c d e f g h i j k l m n o p q r s t u v w x y z

Example
A is the first letter of the alphabet.

L is the .... letter of the alphabet.

B is the .... letter of the alphabet.

Z is the .... letter of the alphabet.

D is the .... letter of the alphabet.

T is the .... letter of the alphabet.

P is the .... letter of the alphabet.

V is the .... letter of the alphabet.

C is the .... letter of the alphabet.

H is the .... letter of the alphabet.

N is the .... letter of the alphabet.

2 Complete these sentences with the correct word from the brackets.

1 I can swim very .... (good/well)

2 There's a .... swimming pool at our school. (good/well)

3 I can't hear you. Don't talk so .... (quiet/quietly)

4 Come on. We must leave .... (quick/quickly)

5 That's a very .... song. (nice/nicely)

6 You sang it very .... (nice/nicely)

3 Complete the list of months.

January ....

....

....

....

....

....

4 How do we say these dates? Write them in full.

27 June ....

2 June ....

3 June ....

5 Write the correct prepositions.

1 I get up .... 9 o'clock .... Sundays.

2 She was born .... 1960.

3 I'm having a party .... 23 December.

4 The film starts .... 3.30 .... the afternoon.

5 My birthday is .... March.

Check your answers with a partner. If there is anything you do not understand, ask your teacher or check in the Grammar reference section on pages 109–114 of your Student's Book.

Revision crossword

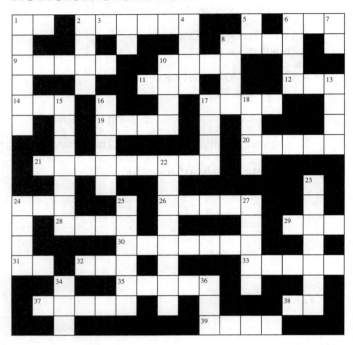

Clues

ACROSS
1 'I'm' is the short from of I ___ .
2 the past tense of 'fight'
6 a young person
8 I was ___ in 1987.
9 This is green.
10 You can sing very ___ .
11 Oh look! there's Michael Douglas. Do you like ___ ?
12 Lucy Loxley ___ in love with Thomas Mowbray.
14 the past tense of 'see'
17 When did you go to London? We ___ yesterday.
19 I come ___ at 4 o'clock every day.
20 ___ do you live?
21 Britain has a queen, but America has a ___ .
24 You write with this.
26 the past tense of 'can'
28 Lord Good ___ the Golden Cat to Cindy.
29 ___ you see Terry yesterday?
30 a small house
31 ___ is short for television.
32 We went to France three years ___ .
33 You wear these inside your shoes.
35 September is the ___ month of the year.
37 the past tense of 'find'
38 I'm sorry. It's all ___ fault.
39 Where ___ you born?

DOWN
1 the eighth month of the year
2 The opposite of 'slow'.
3 Wake ___ !
4 Where are my clothes? I can't find ___ .
5 Let's ___ swimming.
6 What's on at the cinema? I don't ___ .
7 ___ you like Batman?
8 She's got blond hair and ___ eyes.
10 husband and ___
13 I need ___ money.
15 Terry is ___ Sue's coat.
16 The Grey Lady is a ___ .
17 Do you ___ to go to the movies?
18 I heard about the robbery on the ___ .
22 the opposite of 'boring'
23 Hurry. We must leave ___ .
24 You buy stamps at the ___ office.
25 first, ___ , third
27 Only women and girls wear this.
34 I missed the bus yesterday, because I ___ up late.
36 ___ do you do.